Karaoke

D0954584

Karaoke

The Global Phenomenon

Zhou Xun and Francesca Tarocco

reaktion books

Published by Reaktion Books Ltd
33 Great Sutton Street
London EC1V ODX
www.reaktionbooks.co.uk

First published 2007

Printed and bound in China by Toppan Printing Co. Ltd.

British Library Cataloguing in Publication Data
Xun, Zhou
     Karaoke: the global phenomenon
     1. Karaoke
     I. Title II. Tarocco, Francesca
     306.4'842

ISBN-13: 978 1 86189 300 0

Contents

Introduction

Over Christmas 2002, karaoke machines were selling like hot cakes in Britain, and Woolworths stores constantly ran out of stock. From Paris to Toronto, from Iceland to Brazil, even in the heights of the Pyrenees, people are passionate about karaoke. If Bob Costas thought it ridiculous to find himself reading on NBC the news story 'Lebanon has never won an Olympic medal, but recently a Lebanese woman won the Karaoke World Championship in Finland, singing the 1980s classic "Fame"',[1] he would probably be amazed by a search on Google for the word 'karaoke': in September 2005 this produced more than 17.8 million hits. In recent years, karaoke has caught the eye of photographers and featured regularly in film, theatre, literature and the fine arts, from the late British author Dennis Potter's television play *Karaoke*, written in 1994, to the Korean artist Bul Lee's karaoke installation *Cyborgs and Karaoke* (2002), in which karaoke came to symbolize a 'global' fusion culture.[2] Perhaps its best-known appearance is in Sofia Coppola's Oscar-winning film *Lost in Translation*, one of the biggest hits of 2003: suddenly everyone in the audience wanted to join Bill Murray in singing karaoke to Roxy Music's 'More Than This'. The film's soundtrack, with a mix of new and old songs from the United States, France, Japan and Britain, climbed to the top of the charts in 2004, and the Karaoke-kan (a chain of karaoke boxes) where Charlotte (Scarlett Johansson) took Bob (Bill Murray) became a popular tourist haunt in Tokyo's Shibuya district.[3] The world is now witnessing a massive karaoke explosion: it is no longer exclusively an Asian phenomenon, but rather a global phenomenon.

Although many like to view it as an essentially Japanese product, karaoke in the United States bears little resemblance to karaoke in Japan. Like many other phenomena usually defined as 'global', from the internet to McDonald's, karaoke is complex. It blurs many existing boundaries, definitions and categories developed by specialists in cultural and media studies. It does not quite fit into any of the models that anthropologists and ethnomusicologists have tried to deploy. It challenges the view, popularly held in global studies, according to which the USA stands at the centre of global relations, thus equating 'globalization' with 'Americanization'.

For centuries a constant flow of people, ideas and things have moved across the face of the earth and the oceans. In modern times the frequency and speed of such movements have increased greatly with the advent of a global economy, assisted by modern technologies and, of course, by the global network. While all roads might lead to America, the traffic has never been one way. The invasion of the Big Mac and Coca-Cola is only one side of the story, since the world today, from New York to Marrakech, even to a remote Druze village in occupied Palestine, is packed with things made in China. The explosion of karaoke around the world shows that 'global traffic' goes in all directions, crossing multiple

Karaoke Kungfu at Chinese New Year, Malaysia.

Karaoke Indian style.

spaces, at different levels, through different media: from cable wires to the internet, from long-distance tour buses to city taxis, on boats or on aeroplanes, from giant television screens to tiny mobile phones, through the global market or the illicit traffic in counterfeits. Karaoke thus has no centre or periphery, but is rather an interactive global network with constant movement.

This unstoppable global movement has brought about endless circulation, domestication and recycling of objects and technologies, as well as the spread, adaptation and appropriation of cultures and ideas, which frequently offend the guardians of cultural barriers.[4] The notion of 'hybridity' and the illusion of 'authenticity' are in most cases invalid. Transformation and adulteration have always been the norm: the 'indigenous' or the 'original' are but recent inventions. The development and changing face of karaoke in different parts of the world clearly illustrates this. From the islands of the Philippines to the highlands of Canada, local people are endlessly incorporating karaoke into their existing cultural traditions or ways of living.

As a complex, multifaceted, global phenomenon, karaoke should not be conceived in a linear fashion. As John Urry argues, a minor cause may lead to an unprecedented major effect, and the same 'cause' can in specific circumstances produce quite different outcomes.[5] Many factors or agents have contributed to karaoke's spread, its adaptation and inculturation. This is not to discard historical continuity, although without careful examination of each specific set of circumstances it would be unhelpful, and mostly inaccurate, to presume 'historical continuity' as the uniform cause of any historical event. In the case of karaoke, the small innovation that put karaoke online has led to its becoming part of a global network. More importantly, it has changed its nature, since it is no longer a mere machine or a simple act of singing. The network has turned karaoke into a complex organizational system, within which the necessary skills and structures have developed to allow even more technological innovations and potential developments.

Furthermore, the spread and development of karaoke challenges the 'trickle down' theory. In the most fluid fashion, karaoke moves in and out of cultures and spaces, from youth to church, from working-class pubs to fashionable clubs, from charities to brothels, from streets to schools, from cities to villages. There are limitations and there are boundaries – some governments have even attempted to ban karaoke. And yet, like a fluid, karaoke can take different forms as it rushes and trickles through any particular region, mostly managing to overcome all obstacles.

In time and space, karaoke can mean very different things to different people. It is a machine, a tangible object, a cool thing to have and do, a status symbol. It is an illusion, a fantasy dream in an artificial chamber. While it encourages egalitarianism in countries like America ('If the boss can make it out like Paul McCartney, so can I'), in cultures based on a hierarchical system, such as East Asia, it has served as an instrument of homemade democracy. There it is even used as a method for learning foreign languages and improving literacy: a Spanish language teacher in Taiwan reported how, after he started to use the sing-along method, pupils rushed to sign up to his class to enjoy a two-hour singing session in Spanish.[6] More recently, karaoke has inspired a 'mini novel' contest in China, where amateur writers are encouraged to submit their 350-word novels by text message. According to Yu Hua, the well-known Chinese writer, the competition 'is like bringing karaoke to literature. Before the invention of karaoke, only a few people could or would sing in public. Thanks to karaoke, anyone and everyone can sing in public whenever they feel like it. Now thanks to the mobile phone, the same is true with writing.'[7] As a popular medium, karaoke can be an illicit activity or a state-sponsored event. It may be used both as a tool for organizational propaganda or as a means for self-expression. It is a mass culture without being 'mainstream'; there are a few 'karaoke celebrities' yet all who participate are stars. It may be an entertainment, or a way of life; a pleasure, or a real pain. While some have argued that, as a form of modern technology, the karaoke machine can enslave individuals and create alienation, others claim that karaoke has liberated them from the DVD and computer screen and turned them into social animals. China, where a large percentage of the population spent much of its time in recent years watching DVDs, has seen a resurgence of karaoke culture driven by those who feel that karaoke is a more sociable thing to do.

As well as being individuals, participants in karaoke belong to complex interacting social groups, so it may not be helpful to use oversimplified terms such as 'ethnicity' and 'multiculturalism'. Morlam karaoke in Southeast Asia, for instance, even if rooted in the traditional music of the Issan people, is certainly not 'ethnic' music but a popular music widely loved by the urban youth in Bangkok. On the other hand karaoke culture in Britain shows that 'multiculturalism' is by and large a fabricated myth. Most of Britain remains extremely parochial, even in cosmopolitan London, where there is a limited amount of social and cultural mixing. For the majority of British people, however, 'multicultural' means nothing more than consuming the same brands, eating in the latest 'in' restaurants, hanging out in the 'coolest' bar, listening to a mishmash of 'world music', singing karaoke in an artificial paradise and pretending to be someone you are not.

Today there are almost as many different kinds of karaoke venues as there are karaoke songs. In Japan, as in the rest of East Asia, people like to sing at 'karaoke boxes', known as *noraebang* or 'song room' in Korea.

Doors to 'karaoke boxes' in Tokyo.

A variety of karaoke boxes in East Asia.

A selection of karaoke rooms on offer from a karaoke bar in Kurume, Japan.

These are small, or not so small, rooms for hire equipped with karaoke screens, digital machinery, couches and coffee tables. In China there are modern high-rise establishments, devoted exclusively to karaoke, containing hundreds of identical 'karaoke television rooms' or KTV. These can range from relatively cheap and simply furnished rooms, for users content with home-style karaoke technology, to lavishly decorated private lounges replete with the latest high-tech facilities. Most hotels also offer karaoke facilities, both in the form of karaoke rooms and/or karaoke bars. In some parts of Asia karaoke fans can also sing to their hearts' content on trains, buses, boats or even in their own cars. In Europe and North America, too, karaoke venues vary widely, with standard bars, cafes or pubs, quasi-Chinese or Japanese karaoke lounges in London and Brussels, and restaurants-cum-karaoke in Paris. Recently, British and American Christians

The Red Room, Lucky Voice Karaoke, London.

have turned to 'ecclesiastical karaoke', singing along in church to the tunes of 'digital hymnals'.[8] In New York, in a project entitled 'God Given Talent: Epiphityic Architecture and the Trans-spectacular Karaoke Box', Brett Schultz invented a portable structure designed to facilitate 'rooftop karaoke parties' on the thousands and thousands of square metres of unused rooftop space.[9]

Everywhere karaoke creates its own culture, while at the same time reflecting the wider cultural zeitgeist. As the anthropologist Alain Anciaux, a keen karaoke singer, points out in his e-book, every karaoke place has its own 'tribe' or, as some of his interviewees put it, 'its own family'.[10] Undoubtedly, those who visit the same karaoke venue weekly in pursuit of the delicate and thrilling balance between personal satisfaction and collective enjoyment seem to develop great camaraderie with their fellow singers as well as a sense of ownership for the place where they can enjoy their favourite form of leisure. The infamous New Union Pub, one of the original gay-friendly venues in Manchester's 'Gay Village' – the popular television series *Queer as Folk* was filmed on its doorstep – may not look like very much, with its scruffy interiors and bare wooden floors, but every Wednesday night it comes alive with the voices and passionate performances of dozens of proficient singers. The Union enjoys one of the friendliest and most diverse mixture of regular punters we have ever seen: skinny university students from all parts of the world, heavy drinking local couples, flamboyant transvestites – including the large evening's compère – and even bespectacled young professionals in their working suits all love to sing there.

In this book we have attempted to address the complexity of karaoke by exploring its emergence in post-war Japan, its development and its spread across the world in modern times to become a global phenomenon. From Japan to East Asia and Southeast Asia, from North America to Europe, from religion to technology, we have tried to cover as wide a geographical scope and range of topics as possible, and show some of the different meanings associated with karaoke in different contexts. We have used a broad range of source material,

An outdoor karaoke venue in Kiev, Ukraine.

Karaoke in Gorki Park, Krasnoyarsk region.

Winter warmer: karaoke party in a sauna, Russia.

from printed literature to personal interviews and private accounts, to the World Wide Web. We have also included a large number of images as an integral part of the book.

There are of course many countries we have not covered, such as Russia, where karaoke is extremely popular. This is partly due to linguistic limitations and partly to avoid repetition. This book is not an encyclopaedia of karaoke, nor it is a *Lonely Planet* guide to karaoke around the world. It is a cultural study emphasizing its development, spread, social transformation and effect in different parts of the world. Alongside studies of other phenomena, such as disease, tourism, brands and logos, drugs, technologies, and material culture, the study of karaoke provides us with a lens to look at issues of lifestyle, habits of consumption, identity and gender in a global perspective.

Who Invented Karaoke?

Del Rosario versus Inoue

In January 1993 Roberto del Rosario filed a complaint to the *Regional Trial Court* at Makati, Philippines, for patent infringement against the Janito Corporation, the Chinese firm that claimed to have invented the Miyata Karaoke™ machine. Del Rosario alleged that he was a patentee of audio equipment and had improved what was commonly known as the sing-along system or karaoke. He described his sing-along system as a handy, multi-purpose, compact machine that incorporated an amplifier, speaker, one or two tape mechanisms, an optional tuner or radio and a microphone mixer with features to enhance one's voice, such as echo or reverb to simulate opera or a studio sound. The whole system was then encased in a cabinet. He stated that he had developed the system in 1975 and began to market it in 1978. On 15 March 1996 the Supreme Court in the Philippines ruled in favour of Del Rosario, making him the world's sole patent holder for the karaoke system.[1]

Del Rosario's claim further muddled the already complicated origins of karaoke. As with the Bible, there are many accounts regarding the genesis of karaoke. The most common belief is that karaoke originated in Japan, since the term is an abbreviated compound of two Japanese words: 'kara', from *karappo* ('empty'), and 'oke', an abbreviation for *oke-sutura* ('orchestra'). Toru Mitsui, however, explains that the original term karaoke in Japanese does not mean 'empty orchestra', but instead should be understood as 'the orchestra on the recording is void of vocals', referring to the karaoke machine as well as to the singing.[2]

In 1996, about the time the Supreme Court in the Philippines was anointing Del Rosario as the inventor of the karaoke system, a Singapore-based all-karaoke TV channel 'discovered' an amiable-looking character named Inoue Diasuke, from Nishinomiya in Hyogo prefecture, Japan, and made him the 'Grand Daddy' of karaoke.

In 1971 Inoue was a none-too-successful 30-year-old keyboard and vibraphone back-up player in a bar in Kobe. He was, however, much loved by many amateur singers since he seemed to possess a magic touch: his ability to make even a poor singer sing in tune, which later earned him the nickname of a 'human karaoke machine'. Inoue was in such high demand that he had to clone himself. One day a customer asked him to go on a company trip and play for him during a party. Inoue was too busy to go, so he recorded the backup music on a tape and gave it to his customer. According to Inoue, 'That guy was worse than your typical bad singer. He couldn't hit the notes, couldn't even hold a beat. So I purposely recorded the song off-beat. And you know what? He was very happy with the results!' The businessman delivered an emotional rendition of Frank Nagai's 'Leaving Haneda Airport on a 7.50 pm Flight', Inoue collected his money in absentia and came up with another brilliant idea: 'As for me, I couldn't play well without looking at the sheet music, and new songs kept coming out one after the other, so I thought maybe a machine could make things easier for me. In a sense, my invention came about because I was too lazy to learn new songs!' Inoue asked for help from three friends: an electronics specialist, a woodworker and a furniture finisher. Within three months they made him a karaoke machine, a more sophisticated clone of Inoue, complete with microphone and echo effect. They called it the '8-Juke'. By depositing a 100-yen coin into the machine, the backup music would start playing in just five seconds. Initially they made only eleven machines, but they quickly became so popular that they had to produce another ten thousand.[3]

In 1999 *Time* magazine astonishingly named Inoue one of the twentieth century's most influential Asians, arguing that he 'had helped to liberate legions of the once unvoiced: as much as Mao Zedong or Mohandas Gandhi changed Asian days, Inoue transformed its nights.'[4] In 2004,

described in similar terms as 'thereby providing an entirely new way for people to learn to tolerate each other', he was presented at Harvard University with the Ig Nobel Peace Prize, a semi-serious award presented by real Nobel Prize winners.[5] Inoue has also been the subject of films, the most recent one of which, simply called *Karaoke*, features a much better-looking actor than the plump, shortish Inoue. 'At least they got someone tall to play me', he laughs. As for his monumental contribution to the human race, Inoue is less enthusiastic. 'I'm not an inventor', he told journalist David McNeill in a recent interview, 'I simply put things that already existed together, which is completely different. I took a car stereo, a coin box and a small amp to make the karaoke. Who would even consider patenting something like that?'

Inoue now makes a living by selling an eco-friendly detergent and a cockroach repellent for karaoke machines: 'Cockroaches get inside the machines, build nests, and chew on the wires . . . this is the reason why more than 80 per cent of the machines break down.' This is not the first time he has partly profited from the revenues produced by the karaoke industry. In the 1980s he ran a company that successfully persuaded dozens of small production firms to lease songs for 8-Juke karaoke machines, but the introduction of new laser and dial-up technology left him jobless until he discovered that cockroaches, too, love karaoke.[6]

In order to make karaoke into an authentic Japanese story, Wikipedia has attributed its origin to the long tradition of singing and dancing in rural Japan, which dates back to ancient times, or to *Noh*, a major form of musical drama that has been performed since the fourteenth century. The emphasis on singing and dancing in a samurai's training is also thought to have contributed to the development of karaoke. During the Taisho period (1912–26) the *Utagoe Kissa* (song coffee shop), where customers often sang to a live band, became popular.[7] Another popular story claims that, years later, when a strolling guitarist failed to appear, a snack bar owner in Kobe put on tapes of music and asked people if they wanted to sing.[8]

The Welsh revival

Then there are other stories: even the Welsh have jumped on the band-wagon, insisting that they are the inventors of karaoke. The webmaster of a colourful website called 'Wales, The Land of Song' makes bold claims about the 'true' origins of karaoke:

> [W]hat makes Wales really famous for being the Land of Song is that if you gather two or three Welsh people together, in a few minutes there will be talk of singing, even if the singing hasn't started already! The Japanese are the ones who invented the Karaoke Machine, but it is the Welsh that invented Karaoke itself, hundreds and hundreds of years ago! Singing heartily in public is a new thing in Japan, but a very old tradition in Wales! Furthermore, the Welsh feel no need for alcoholic stimulants to induce the courage to start singing![9]

While one might find such a statement dubious, it is certainly true that Welsh people love to sing in public. By the seventeenth century public hymn singing had already emerged in Wales, largely due to the effort of Nonconformists such as William Wroth, Walter Cradock and Vavasor Powell. All three were travelling evangelists, who advocated hymn singing in

Welsh chapels as a useful tool in building fellowship within the community and a means of witnessing to others outside. Some even called public hymn singing 'the most dynamic preacher and recruiter of them all'. Singing hymns in public was also believed to help believers focus on their faith.

Until the end of the Second World War the Methodist hymns became practically the only form of music known to much of the population in parts of Wales. Other traditional forms of music, folk dancing, games and customs effectively vanished, except in North Wales, where they were preserved by a few gypsy families.[10]

From carol singing to the music hall

While public hymn singing was an integral part of the Methodist Revival, which became a defining aspect of Welsh life, across the border in Puritan England public hymn singing, or any forms of music except for metrical psalms, was officially banned in church. It was not until 1820 that the Church of England officially authorized hymn singing. Although public singing and music were not allowed, it is believed that during this time the Elizabethan tradition of singing Christmas carols survived in secret in some remote villages in England. In the 1830s William Sandys and Davies Gilbert travelled around collecting these survivors and published them in a series of volumes. They included such later favourites as 'God rest you merry, gentlemen', 'The first Nowell' and 'I saw three ships', the last of which has a very optimistic tone and is considered to be one of the most upbeat and celebratory melodies of the winter season.[11]

As a matter of fact, centuries ago people in Europe began to celebrate the winter solstice with public singing and dancing. Most of songs were joyful in tone, intended to raise the spirits. Early Christians took on this essentially pagan practice from around AD 129 and introduced the 'Angel's Hymn' ('Gloria in excelsis'), replacing the pagan festivities with their own celebrating Christ's birth. These early Christmas hymns were mostly sung in Latin, however, and held little attraction for the general public, most of whom did not understand their words. It was not until after 1223, when St Francis of Assisi introduced nativity plays in Italy, that Christmas carols began to spread across Europe to France, Spain, Germany and elsewhere. Normally, the actors in such plays would tell the story in songs and many of the choruses were in a language the audience could understand. Most of the early Christmas carols in the Elizabethan period were loosely based on the Christmas story and were seen as a form of entertainment rather than as specifically religious. They were mostly performed by travelling singers and minstrels, who often changed the words to suit the local audience.

When Cromwell and the Puritans came to power during the 1640s, Christmas carols were banned, together with other forms of music, although this did not suppress people's desire to sing. Post-Puritan England saw a proliferation of mass singing in public. An early demonstration of this phenomenon came during the Handel festival in 1791, when hundreds of singers gathered together in Westminster Abbey for a performance of *Messiah*. The Halifax Choral Society was founded in 1817, followed by the Bradford Choral Society in 1821 and the Huddersfield Choral Society in 1836. All three were formed in local public houses, and since then British pubs have become a favourite venue for public singing. Meanwhile, from London to the remote English countryside, every village and every town formed its own choral group. There is no doubt singing in public was a much loved pastime in the nineteenth century. The Crystal Palace, built for the London Great Exhibition of 1851, soon became one of the grandest and most popular venues for choral concerts.[12]

As an alternative to pubs, beer halls and gin palaces, many mass music halls were erected for the entertainment of 'respectable' audiences in urban cities. A typical music hall song consists of a series of verses, sung by the performer alone, and a repeated chorus carrying the principal melody, and the audience is encouraged to join in. By the turn of the twentieth century it was claimed that the population of England was divided into two categories: 'Those who sing and those who do not.' As Nigel Fountain has shown in his recent book on mass entertainment in Edwardian England, by 1899, when the New Bedford Palace of Varieties first opened its doors in Camden Town, Britain was literally an empire of music halls stretching from Shoreditch to Sunderland.[13]

Originally a working-class entertainment, by the first decade of the twentieth century, the music hall had become a cultural norm in Britain with royal approval: in 1912 King George V attended the first Royal Variety Performance (then styled the Royal Command Performance) at the Palace Theatre on Cambridge Circus in London. While the peak of the music hall era was probably during the First World War, its type of entertainment remained popular into the 1950s. Other forms of popular entertainment, however, rose to prominence from the 1920s and '30s, its biggest competitor being the cinema, but the spread of television in the early 1950s sealed the fate of the music hall.

Even after music halls lost their appeal, public singing did not. The rise of cinema provided a new media for public singing, from which came a form of sing-along. Long before the days of 'Sing-along-a *Sound of Music*' screenings or the appearance of karaoke, cinema audiences in Chengdu, the largest city in China's southwest frontier region, were already singing along with their favourite stars during the late 1930s. Partly owing to its geographical isolation, Chengdu was largely a backward-looking city, where people had a very reserved attitude towards anything new. From 1937, however, the Sino-Japanese War changed this forever. Surrounded by

Beer bottles and karaoke are inseparable: a man singing karaoke at Taichung Park, Taiwan. Note his shirt that matches the tiled wall.

steep mountains – the famous Chinese poet Li Bai once wrote that to reach Chengdu and its surrounding areas was as impossible as to reach heaven – the city was spared the Japanese invasion. War refugees flooded into the city and China's leading universities relocated to Chengdu. The many students brought with them new fashions, tastes and novelties from the coastal cities, and turned Chengdu into an entertainment hub. Until the end of the Second World War the city was the most happening place in China. A number of cinemas, still a relatively new entertainment in China, sprang up. In order to lure the public, the cinemas had constantly to innovate their offerings. The Daguanming cinema, for example, invited local translators to give spontaneous translations of foreign films, often using

humorous expressions or local slang to make the audience laugh: translation was part of the show. The Guomin cinema in the city centre provided a sing-along facility by projecting the words of popular tunes onto the screen. This was popular with young people who wanted to emulate famous stars such as Zhou Xuan, Li Lihua and Bai Guang.[14] Decades later, Chengdu was to become one of the first cities outside Japan to embrace karaoke. This was partly because anything from Japan was seen as prestigious, and partly because it fitted right into an existing local culture where people love to socialize.

It would be arbitrary to suggest that karaoke has evolved from the hymn-singing culture in Wales or the public singing culture in England, although as a modern medium it has helped to revive the British passion

Two men enjoy karaoke on the bank of River Yangtze, Sichuan, China.

'Praying to a karaoke goddess': a mad karaoke party but a good time, San Francisco.

Abba karaoke at Chapter Arts, Cardiff.

for singing, much as it speeded up social bonding in Chengdu. Today karaoke has become part of the local cultural traditions and a way of life. While one might claim that it is a quintessentially Japanese product, it has, however, struck a chord with audiences worldwide. As Pico Iyer observes:

> Signs for 'Karaoke nights' appear outside mom-and-pop stalls in Third World villages and on the glittery billboard of the Hollywood Park Casino in California. Global icons practice it in films like *My Best Friend's Wedding*, and steelworkers howl away in English towns, where 'carry-okie' sounds like a cousin of 'cash 'n' carry'. Religious figures have been heard to say that Karaoke is as essential to the soul as

Tai Chi. It feels like 53 million Japanese have all inflicted their voices upon the world. Today, even in a city like Phnom Penh you can sing everything from 'O Sole Mio' to 'Rudolph the Red-Nosed Reindeer'.[15]

Topless waitresses at a karaoke night in Finland.

Yet, as mentioned in the Introduction, in each of these places karaoke adopts different features and characteristics, and takes on cultural-specific meanings and symbolisms. In China, for instance, karaoke is a strong tie that binds the family together in an age when the generation gap and the pressures of modern life have become a threat to the traditional extended family structure. While karaoke relieves stress in many trying to cope with the pressures of modern life, it can equally be a means to divert boredom in rural societies. It has also been used as an educational tool, and entered the public school system in Japan and South-east Asia. Many young Asians

Karaoke night in Coates Bar, London.

go to karaoke venues in order to learn English by singing, as well as the local popular songs, Western pop songs. In Britain and parts of North America, where people used to sing together around a piano, karaoke has now found its way into the existing bar and pub culture.

'Karaoke Fever': Japan and Korea

Karaoke, the Japanese success

Karaoke emerged in Japan in the late 1970s and early '80s at a time when the country was trying to rediscover its place in the world. It was also a period of enormous economic growth and Japanese products and technologies were taking over the world, thanks to manufacturers' ability in making and mass marketing their goods, as well as continuously changing and refashioning them in order to attract a wide range of consumers. One of the key factors in the success of Japanese goods is not that they are big and impressive, but rather that, from the Sony Walkman to the video games of Nintendo and Sega and to Bandai's Tamagotchi, they are portable, functional, affordable and personal. These small machines make convenience fun and fun convenient. Japanese technologies have empowered the 'little guy': 'suddenly anyone can listen to his or her own music while on a crowded train, fax their handwriting across the globe or perform their own rendition of "I Saw Mommy Kissing Santa Claus"'.[1] Karaoke makes no one marginal.

In 1976 Clarion was the first company in Japan to produce a karaoke machine for business use, but soon it made its way into the mass market as a household item. In the early 1980s, the age of tape and recorders, a basic karaoke set, including a cassette player and pre-recorded tapes, a microphone, echo control and songbook, cost $400. It has been estimated that sales of karaoke home units in Japan in 1982 zoomed to $625 million, more than the figure spent in the United States on gas appliances: so popular did

A patron at a karaoke bar in Tokyo, Japan.

they become that in the following year many of the approximately 22,000
Japanese stores that stocked them sold out. Revenues from karaoke sales
amounted to $10 billion in 1996.[2] Today it is estimated that there are about
50 million karaoke practitioners in Japan, scattered around which are some
14,000 'karaoke box' buildings where groups of singers may rent rooms.

No matter how grand and unbroken a history may be imagined to
frame karaoke culture in Japan, it only emerged there about 30 years ago,
at the peak of the country's economic growth. It first became popular in
bars in the urban areas of Osaka and Kobe, and of the surrounding Kansai

Unstoppable karaoke: karaoke makes the small guy big in Japan.

area, as a typical night-time entertainment for the growing number of 'salary-men' or 'corporate soldiers'. Karaoke bars and nightclubs provided salary-men with a public space, a centre for male conviviality where, after a hard day at work, they could drop in with their colleagues for a few drinks and a good sing.

Most of these bars had a machine not dissimilar to Inoue's '8-Juke', a veritable 'closet Caruso', to use *Time*'s famous definition. After depositing a 100 yen coin, the equivalent of three or four drinks in those days, the machine would turn the music on. The aspirant singer could then find the song in the songbook, pick the microphone up and croon away. Popular accompaniments ranged from work songs of Japanese farmers, through favourite tunes of those who had fought in the Second World War, to 'I Left My Heart in San Francisco'. Karaoke combined with drink served as the ultimate form of stress relief from the tedious monotony of the corporate world. Some even claimed that there was no other entertainment that could make them feel so refreshed, and that utter drunkenness was the best way to end a tiresome day; as the popular saying claims, 'Relax! Relax! and Relax! until total collapse'. This is what karaoke and Budweiser offered them.

The general assumption that 'new trends come from the West of Japan' recognizes the important role of that region, and Kobe in particular, in the history of modern Japan. The country's first supermarket and sauna were established in the Kansai area, and Kansai has created global success stories such as instant noodles and automated ticket barriers. Another saying, 'Fashion comes from Kobe', signals a common belief held by many Japanese that fashion always begins with young women in Kobe before it becomes popular in Tokyo, so fashion magazines have to keep an eye constantly on the women of Kobe. Since its port was opened to international trade in 1868, on the eve of the Meiji Restoration, Kobe has been the centre of international exchange and attracted many Westerners. A jazz festival is held every year in Kitano-cho, the city's former foreign quarter, making Kobe a Mecca for jazz fans from around the world. The Kobe Festival is famous for its parade enlivened with samba rhythms and dance, a tradition that is probably linked with the birth of karaoke in Kobe.[3] Alongside the transnational connection, in the 1970s amateur singing in public to the accompaniment of live bands also became widely popular in the Kobe area. According to Toru Mitsui, this led to the invention of the Crescent Juke, a modified jukebox and prototype of the karaoke machine, much like the one invented by Inoue.[4]

At the time when karaoke was starting to flourish in Kobe, the city also produced an extraordinary woman politician named Takako Doi. An imposing figure (at 168 cm, she is decidedly tall for a Japanese woman), she speaks with great confidence and authority. In a land where unmarried women are considered incomplete, Doi remains steadfastly single. In 1969, when she was still a lecturer at Doshisha University, Doi approached the deputy mayor of Kobe seeking an apology for an inaccurate newspaper report suggesting that she had accepted an invitation from the Japan Socialist Party to run for a Parliamentary seat. According to a report, the official was both condescending and blunt: 'Wouldn't it be really stupid to run in an election you know you have no chance of winning?' Affronted, Doi snapped back, 'I've decided right here, at this very moment, that I will run for this election.' She went on to win and has not lost a single contest since. A good winner in politics, Takako is also a keen karaoke singer, a hobby that won her many supporters. As well as being one of the few women in Japanese politics, she was also among the first few to enter the then still very much male-dominated world of karaoke bars, where she gave an impassioned rendition of Paul Anka's classic 'My Way'.[5] Karaoke gave Japanese women a public voice.

In the 1960s national talent shows were popular on television, with potential singing talents being invited to take part in televised competitions. These shows became inextricably connected to the karaoke culture of later years and, in a way, were essentially forerunners of 'Stars in their Eyes', the popular karaoke show that took British television by storm in the early 1990s. The television shows inspired many Japanese people to '*issho-kemmei ni yatta*', literally 'give it a good try'. The resilience and entrepreneurship that enabled Japan to recover from the Second World War seemed to become part of the karaoke experience. Karaoke was in tune with the Japanese psyche of the post-war era: it was the spirit of 'Yes, you/I can do it!' that propelled Japan's economic boom. Karaoke is therefore of great social and economic significance: it is much more than mere entertainment – it is linked to the spirit of personal and national triumph. Anyone who aspires to the 'Japanese success' aspires to karaoke. All over Japan, great numbers of people took up karaoke singing as a serious hobby.

In as much as it is a cultural product, karaoke is also a product of technological innovation. In Japan the karaoke boom largely resulted from the mass production and mass marketing of the home units. According to a report in *Time* magazine, one top-of-the-line model, costing about $4,000, includes synthesizers that can create a bossa nova or waltz beat, a computerized music memory system and two giant 1.6-metre speakers. For another $1,000, vocalists can add a small black box that grades their singing by scoring how well they stay on pitch and keep time with the beat of the electronic accompaniment.[6]

While on the one hand home units enabled a wider section of the population to practise karaoke, on the other hand, since most Japanese live in small houses with little or no soundproofing, loud singing with a microphone could be the cause of neighbourly discontent, especially in a culture where people greatly value quietness. Thus, in the late 1980s Japanese entrepreneurs created the 'karaoke box', a fully soundproofed room equipped with state-of-the-art technology and graced with sofas and tables, where to have a drink and nibble snacks and sing in front of a big screen. The karaoke box combines the intimacy of a private living room, a small space to be enjoyed with friends and family, with the vibrancy of a public venue. It is generally believed that the first karaoke box appeared in 1984 in a rice field, just west of Kansai, in the countryside of Okayama prefecture: it was a converted truck container.

Other early karaoke boxes were similarly converted from old truck containers set alongside main roads in the suburbs. Karaoke boxes were established mainly to provide a space for singing and as an alternative to bars. They became a social space for female office workers, housewives, students and families. Gradually, however, karaoke boxes of various sizes were introduced in entertainment centres in various cities throughout Japan, catering for singing parties of between two and eight individuals. Arguably, this was one of the driving forces behind the transformation of karaoke into one of Japan's most widespread leisure activities. As the numbers and varieties of participants expanded, so the repertoire widened. The enclosed, intimate space of a karaoke box provided a more relaxed atmosphere than a bar. It is often claimed that it helps strengthen the ties between participants, although Mamika, a girl from Akita, a small town in northern Japan, would dis-

Karaoke, a favourite pastime in Japan.

agree: 'Even though we went in groups I felt very lonely, because no one was listening to the other person singing, everybody was so busy finding a song to sing and to show off in front of the others.'[7]

Ironically, the opportunity to be ostentatious in public explains much of karaoke's appeal. In a culture where the correct level of politeness is given prime importance and modesty is considered a virtue, karaoke provides an opportunity to give one's ego a boost. If vanity is universal, perhaps there is a real need to show off from time to time. The karaoke box not only gives individuals the chance to do so in front of a group, it places participants in charge of the audio and visual equipment, thus giving them the feeling to be 'in control'. In addition, being enclosed in an artificial space allows people to have an entirely new experience of the world, and a pleasurable one at that, rather like the experience of going on holiday.

From a night-time entertainment, karaoke has turned into a national obsession. Young and old, men and women, literally everyone has their favorite Karaoke song, and everyone has a place to karaoke. While McDonald's has introduced low-cost Karaoke-for-Kids together with the official Big Mac Song, to lure housewives some karaoke venues also stock special children's songs, so that kids and their mums can take turns in singing. A toy manufacturer recently launched a karaoke microphone for small children. During the cherry blossom season, when millions of Japanese visit parks and open spaces to view the trees, picnickers haul karaoke appliances onto the lawn and sing to their hearts' content while sipping

Hello Kitty tries to woo families at Tokyo's Big Echo

Years of rapid expansion have left the karaoke box business stuck with overcapacity. About a quarter of the so-called 'boxes' (tiny cubicles furnished with state-of-the-art sound equipment) have been forced to close down in recent years. Thus, in pursuit of a dwindling customer base, the remaining karaoke box companies are fighting a fierce price war, allowing patrons in for pennies or even gratis, in the hope of eking out a slim margin from food and drink sales. At Big Echo, a Tokyo-based karaoke box chain, giant pink pastel Hello Kitty murals have been added to the décor in a bid to attract families, a still underrepresented consumer group. Songs are no longer played via laser disc – regarded almost as medieval technology in Japan – but rather delivered straight from a remote host computer via a broadband internet connection. Songbooks the size of telephone

See, we are in control, that makes us happy! – Cesar, Laura, Emily and a karaoke remote control, Japan.

Karaoke in Japanese.

A karaoke remote control.

directories offer patrons a staggering selection of 30,000 songs. However, there is no real need to use such books, more a nostalgic memento of days gone by, as any selection can be quickly summoned from a touch-screen, hand-held remote. In their attempt to keep clients coming back, karaoke boxes are gradually evolving into game centres, where singers can get their performance rated or have their horoscopes read. Such gimmicks are popular among after-five groups of office workers and even among young couples on their first date.[8]

A room of karaoke machines in Namjatown, Japan. Each machine is about 4 feet tall. Above them are TV monitors for singers to see the lyrics and video.

opposite: A Hello Kitty karaoke box, Tokyo, Japan.

Karaoke at a shrine, Japan.

beer and chewing dried octopus legs. Even Japanese troops on humanitarian missions have to have a karaoke bar at their camp site.[9] The late journalist Hashida Sawako described singing karaoke in the desert as the one thing that kept him sane while working in West Iraq during the Second Gulf War.[10]

Karaoke has become an essential part of Japanese life, so essential that many people even feel duty-bound to visit karaoke venues. In a society dominated to an extent by corporate culture, social acceptance is given prime importance. In many cases karaoke is in fact a compulsory company activity, especially for female staff and new recruits to the company. When Mamika first started to work in a Japanese company, she was forced to attend karaoke venues with her male colleagues after work. How she dreaded those long and endless nights. Apparently, as she remembers, most business deals at her company were made during karaoke sessions.

From a serious hobby, karaoke has turned into a serious business and become a subject of training. Private enterprises known as *kyoshitsu* (karaoke class) emerged to give vocal lessons to aspiring amateur singers. There is a 'Karaoke Corner', a television programme offering professional advice to karaoke singers, books such as *Karaoke Jotatsuho* ('How to Improve your Karaoke'), and even karaoke correspondence courses. Karaoke is performance formalized through a set of instructions. According to William Kelly, such instruction

A karaoke bar for cowboys, Osaka, Japan.

encompasses both technical and social aspects of the performance and is dispensed by acknowledged experts – usually well-known professional singers in the case of television programs and correspondence courses – and semi-professional singers, or trained music and singing teachers in the case of more local forums. The range of instruction and how to advice is extremely broad, covering vocal technique, timing and enunciation of sounds, stage posture, performance style, even

microphone position, and advice in nearly every other imaginable
aspect of self-presentation within the context of singing *karaoke*.[11]

Gender stereotypes are reflected in the instruction. *Josei Seven*, a gos-
sip magazine primarily targeted at middle-aged housewives, recently published an article dispensing a sort of karaoke 'Ten Commandments' for
young women who have just entered the workforce. The article claims that
a distinction should be made between singing karaoke 'for fun' and
singing karaoke in the context of 'after five' leisure (or *tsukiai* in Japanese,
the after-work socializing with company colleagues obligatory among
white collar employees): 'The singing-with-a-friend-on-a-Saturday frame
of mind is not appropriate! From basic manners to what not to sing,
teaching you all the keys to avoiding blunders!' Here are the rules:

1. Listen respectfully to the singing of the boss
2. Practice and be able to sing at least three duet songs so that you are able to accompany your boss on request
3. Take care not to sing the boss's favourite song as he is likely not to be able to sing too many different songs
4. Take care to avoid songs which are likely to have a depressing effect, such as those which are nostalgic or about separation and lost love
5. Take care to avoid songs which are unfamiliar to others since they are more likely to chat during your performance if they do not know the song
6. Avoid sexy songs which are likely to offend senior office ladies
7. Choose a song the boss has heard at least once before
8. Wear a suit rather than a sexy dress out of respect for senior office ladies
9. When not singing, be sure to maintain an awareness of and express an interest in those around you.[12]

Another article entitled 'Utai joozu, kiki joozu: kotsu to mana' (Singing well, listening well: tips and manner), published in the magazine *Shuukan Josei* (Women's Weekly), contains various sketches on the deportment desirable during a karaoke performance.[13] It is suggested that women should stand with one foot placed slightly in front of the other and pointed at an outward angle, one hand holding the microphone at their mouth and the other at their side. Blinking should be avoided, while leaning against a wall, turning and twisting excessively, and putting a hand in one's pocket or on the hip are definitely taboo. Men, on the other hand, according to Kelly,

are advised to stand on the stage square with feet apart at shoulder width, holding the microphone at the mouth with one hand and the microphone cord in the other hand, which should be placed in front of the navel. Even the proper way of holding the microphone is illustrated and described – in one hand, about a cigarette's length from the mouth. Holding the microphone in two hands, or even in one with the smallest finger up as a woman might hold a tea cup are described as unacceptable.[14]

There are proper rules for karaoke, but they are not as easy to follow as one imagines.

Although all this may sound odd to some, press reports of several incidents at karaoke venues suggest that there is perhaps a reason for teaching proper karaoke manners in Japan. A 51-year-old carpenter, for example, was arrested for shooting his drinking companion in an argument over a karaoke song. Shigeru Yoshida was drinking with Genshou Shimajiri, a 53-year-old taxi driver, at a karaoke venue in Yokohama late one night and started arguing over who would sing the next song. The argument led to a fight and, in a moment of rage, Yoshida shot Shimajiri.[15]

Shimajiri is not the only victim of the karaoke craze. A report shows that thousands of people in Japan are suffering from 'karaoke-phobia', fearing the dreaded machine so much that they become ill when faced with one. Toru Yuba, a professional singer, told a paper that around 600 people have turned to him for help. To make matters even worse, a report by Keito University Hospital in Tokyo recently suggested that 10 per cent of patients suffering from throat polyps may have contracted them through singing karaoke.[16]

Deviant behaviour and psychological traumas seemingly linked with karaoke, however, are also a reflection of a wider set of problems existing in Japanese society. Depression, frustration and drunkenness are some of the main manifestations of social discontent, for which karaoke has functioned as a palliative. According to a 1994 study made by a Tokyo police researcher, the number of drunken people in the streets has fallen thanks to karaoke bars. In 1976, the year karaoke became popular in bars, the number of drunks fell by 4,000. In 1982, there was another sharp fall in conjunction with the karaoke 'home boom' in Japan and the introduction of the karaoke box. Explaining these findings to the *Japan*

At a porn karaoke in Hotel Adonis, Osaka, Japan.

http://www.clubdam.com/be

未成年のお客様へ

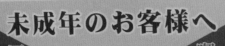

飲　酒　　　　　　　　喫　煙

ダメ！絶対

シンナー等の可燃物・薬物　　　迷惑行為

お守りいただけない場合は直ちに退店して頂き、場合によっては警察に通報致します

　ご利用時間　

16歳未満の方は午後6時まで　　　18歳未満の方は午後10時まで
　　　　　　　　　　　　　　　　　　（保護者同伴の場合は午後11時まで）
学生証等の身分証明書のご提示をお願いする場合があります。

会員カードを受付でゲット！　　Edyチャージャー（入金機）で　　DAMステーション画面にある
　　　　　　　　　　　　　　　会員カードにチャージ（入金）します　スロログインボタンにタッチ

or

おサイフケータイでも
会員になれます

チャージ（入金）は、
会員カードでも
おサイフケータイでもOK。

チャージはカンタン

にタッチ

会員カードを
DAMステーションに
セット

ニックネームと
写真を登録

★自分だけの楽由
★採点結果わかり
★オーディション結
★全国のDAMS
　でも作ったリス

Times, the officer claimed: 'There is no doubt that karaoke, a means to vent frustration, is helping to reduce the number of people who get drunk and lose control of themselves.'[17] However, the report made no mention of the fact that in nearly all karaoke bars Japanese men enjoy singing as much as they indulge in drinking alcohol. As a matter of fact, Japanese men happen to lose control in karaoke bars rather frequently, and this is considered socially acceptable in Japan.

Karaoke has not only helped Japanese society to function 'normally', it has also contributed to economic growth and helped to promote the image of Japan on the international stage. Since the 1870s Japan has participated in world fairs, using them as a key medium through which to affirm its modernity and distinctiveness, as well as assert its place in the international community.[18] In January 1983 Clarion, one of the largest karaoke manufacturers in the world, displayed its latest and best machines at a Las Vegas trade exhibition with great success: the company received orders from American dealers totalling $1 million.

As the market leader in the karaoke industry, Clarion is a major force behind the sale and marketing of karaoke systems, introducing synthesizer karaoke for home and business use with the catchphrase 'Song is communication, karaoke is Clarion'. Clarion is also responsible for making karaoke travel. Today, one can sing karaoke while comfortably seated on a sightseeing bus or onboard a train. Tourists and commuters alike, whether in Langzhong, a remote ancient town in south-west China, or in cosmopolitan Toronto, are never far from a karaoke screen and a microphone.

Keeping abreast of technological developments, Clarion has also pushed the digitalization of karaoke. It is claimed that such technology has gained in popularity because it offers superior operational capacity and durability, and is less likely to malfunction. In today's competitive market, in order to increase sales it is necessary to expand the range of products to suit the market's demands. Thus, Clarion has also introduced the 'karaoke robot' (transportable unitized system) for banquet halls.

Clarion has focused on promoting its products to hotels and luxury resorts throughout Asia. The Grand

Karaoke bus in Taiwan.

InterContinental Hotel in Seoul, for example, uses karaoke as a marketing tool to attract potential customers:

Sing the Night Away
Karaoke at Grand InterContinental Seoul

There is great news for those of you who love to sing – the Karaoke at the Grand InterContinental Seoul (B1) has been completely refurbished. The Karaoke has a total of nine different rooms prepared to accommodate parties of from 4 to 30 persons. The hotel's entire liquor menu is available along with a delicious selection of snacks such as mixed grill with beef tenderloin, pork filet, sausages, and lamb chops; seafood sticks with shrimp and scallops; smoke salmon; blue corn nachos, or even fresh fruit.

Karaoke, Korea's national sport

The Grand InterContinental Hotel in Seoul has certainly pushed the right button. Oh, how the Koreans love to sing! Park Moo-jong, the chief editor of the *Korean Times*, once proudly declared singing the 'national sport' of Korea. On 2 November 2002, in a feature article marking the forthcoming football World Cup, Mr Park warned the huge numbers of visitors that they'd better acquire a fondness for singing:

If World Cup visitors from abroad have a liking for song, they may fit right in with their Korean hosts. An invitation to a dinner party, even a formal one, may demand stamina and a shedding of reserve. They may be expected, called on, urged and almost required to stand up on their own and 'sing'.[19]

Korea, the 'Land of the Morning Calm', has a great singing tradition, according to Mr Park, and has produced many great singers from Sumi Jo to Shin Young-ok and Hong Hye-kyung. Almost every Korean, he claimed, has a fair-to-good-to-excellent singing voice, and 'even the few who might experience pitch problems or turn up tone deaf will struggle on valiantly, eliciting enthusiastic responses from the sympathetic audience.' In order to appreciate this cultural characteristic of his countrymen and to share their music experience, Mr Park urged all visitors to visit a *noraebang* – a routine social activity in Korea.[20]

Noraebang literally means 'song room'. Many Koreans claim that the karaoke box originated in Korea, not Japan, although *noraebang* became popular only in the late 1980s, around the time of the Seoul Olympics (1988). *Noraebang* soon became a major entertainment venue for Koreans, 'because people really love to sing and use them to relieve stress and kill time.' One of the first things a visitor to Korea would notice today is that *noraebang* are everywhere: even the smallest neighbourhoods now boast a variety of karaoke venues. Most *noraebang* provide good space at low cost for people to sing out their daily stress, while strengthening solidarity among friends, company colleagues, family members or people they meet for the first time on business. Politicians, government officials, business executives, office workers, students, clerks, housewives, doctors – it is claimed that once Koreans find themselves holding a microphone at a *noraebang* they are seldom shy or afraid of performing in front of others.

There are two types of *noraebang*. The first is the family-orientated singing room in which alcohol is prohibited. At such venues, entire families can be seen attempting to 'harmonize current pop songs together, teenagers bond over the latest romantic heartthrob's production, and children run wild murdering Korean nursery rhymes'.[21] The second type of *noraebang* is one where patrons are allowed to drink alcohol. It was only in the 1990s that the Ministry of Health and Welfare allowed karaoke lounges and bars to sell alcohol. It is thought that alcohol serves as a recreational lubricant, helping singers to 'loosen up their tonsils for the proper vocalization of their favourite Tom Jones, Beatles or Frank Sinatra classics'.[22] Most of these alcohol-friendly karaoke clubs often crawl with students, locals or expatriates after a night out on the town. They are sometimes referred to as *dallanjujom*, literally 'happy drinking house'. While most *noraebang* look pretty plain and simple, there are also some really fancy karaoke lounges or bars with superb

In a *noraebang*,
Korea.

audio systems and large-screen videos.

Fancy or plain, almost all *noraebang* offer the same selection of songs, with a rather limited supply of older foreign songs. Songs are numbered and all the *noraebang* use the same numbering system. A typical *noraebang* is equipped with a fat book full of song selections in multiple languages.

Individuals take turns picking their favourite songs to sing in front of others.
Most karaoke singers are said to have one song that they are especially
good at, and which they use to show off their singing abilities. This is
their *Ohako* ('18th'), which originally referred to the eighteen most popular
Japanese kabuki plays. The term was adapted in Korea during the Japanese
colonial period and is now slang in Korean for being good at an entertainment such as dancing, singing or playing an instrument.

Contemporary Korean vocal music ranges from traditional *pansori*
(epics that last for several hours) to syrupy, ballad-laden country music (by
post-Korean War celebrities such as Na-Hoon-na and Nam-jin), and a variety of pop bands, many of which often display a disturbing fondness for
bad English acronyms (HOT, SES, GOD, BOA). Modern youth music, known
as K-Pop, is, according to Ken May, a keen observer of East and South-east
Asian youth culture,

> uninhibited by western concepts such as artistic integrity. The high-
> gloss performers often lip-synch in concert, appear on silly television
> shows, and blatantly endorse products in advertisement campaigns.
> The Korean music industry is unhindered by the western idea that
> payola is somehow dishonest. The corporate star-making industry
> has repeatedly been caught paying bribes in trade of guest spots on
> television or radio programs. K-Pop has the metallic taste of industri-
> alization. Performers are corporate assembled commodities. Singers
> often have little say in writing music or choosing the uniforms they
> wear on stage. Manufactured boy band singers are even prevented
> from having girlfriends in order to preserve the wholesome boy-next-
> door image.[23]

This being the case, it is not a great leap for Koreans to embrace
karaoke. The style, computer-programmed, artificial and rejecting live
instruments, is only one step away from what Korean youths listen to on
their iPods every day. Karaoke in Korea is sometimes compared to a
'nationwide amateur singing contest' to the accompaniment of a videotape or laser disc. It gives everyone the chance to be a star, even if it is

only for one evening at an insulated local singing room, and even if one might be their only audience. There is even a type of karaoke booth in which one can sit alone or with a friend, singing along to a videotape or laser disk, and record their performance for around W12,000 (approx. $11) per hour.

DDR, 'Digital Dance Revolution' (perhaps better known as Dance Dance Revolution), is another national sport in Korea. This video game, originating in Japan, has become extremely popular in Korea and China since the late 1990s. While it has begun to fizzle out in China, it remains strong in Korea and is currently a big hit among teenagers in south London. The game consists of a large floor pad marked with arrows that light up in sequence to the music. It can be hooked up to a home computer, Sony PlayStation or TV (there is even a dedicated DDR channel broadcast in Korea). The object of the game is to jump or stamp on the arrow when it lights up in time to the music. Since it is sometimes necessary to move very fast, DDR has been recommended as a good form of exercise to lose weight.

While many have their own DDR pad at home, most young people in Korea prefer to go out on the streets where there are coin-operated DDR machines. DDR arcade halls may be found on almost every street corner. In DDR karaoke booths one can sing as well as dance: as the spaces on the screen light up, dancers jump on them in time to the music, singing karaoke at the same time.

Karaoke has taken Korea by storm and become an important feature in its everyday life. According to a short essay that Heri Lim, a primary school student from Korea, wrote to introduce his country to his friends in Oregon:

Seoul is a beautiful and really popular and fashionable city. There are lots of places to have fun, like Video rooms, and Karaoke . . . I liked to go to Karaoke with friends . . . Korea is famous for Tae Kwon Do. Korea had the 1988 Olympics. The Korean people love to have fun and sing Karaoke and go shopping.[24]

Some even claim that karaoke has improved Koreans' literacy rate and foreign language skills. English lyrics are sometimes displayed by video monitor while the students practice pronunciation. It is suggested that even the shyest students in the ESL classroom seem to open up once they hit the karaoke club. Ken May, who used to teach English in Korea, has often been surprised by how his students could deliver a song in impeccable English, even though they might stumble over basic sentences in class. Even some of the worst-behaved Korean schoolchildren snap into shape when given the opportunity to sing during class. The misspelling of English lyrics is, however, a regular feature. Ken May fondly remembers the extraordinary epiphany that took place at a *noraebang* where he sang his heart out:

> I was enthusiastically singing a Sex Pistols song – 'Anarchy in the UK' – standing on a chair and dramatically slamming a tambourine against a wall, when the apple of enlightenment dropped out from the ceiling and stuck me squarely on the head. It sounded exactly like an oven timer going off, 'ding'! The Sex Pistols do not play the tambourine, nor do they carefully read lyrics off a television monitor to get a higher score. The synthetic music blared without drums, guitar, or a bass line. Like a background tune in an elevator or an unobtrusive supermarket ditty, the classic Punk Rock song lulled me with its computer-programmed single keyboard melody. The microphone heavily echoed with reverb that conveniently disguised my atrocious singing. On the monitor screen – which simultaneously displayed Asian women in bikinis – incorrect and misspelled lyrics briefly scrolled down: 'I am an anti-Chris / I dont know what I want / But I know how to get it / I want to destroy passer buy / I want to be an anarchy'.[25]

The Korean enthusiasm for karaoke sometimes shocks visitors from abroad. Jeff Shields, another ex-English teacher in Korea, once visited the holy site of Kyong-ju, the home of some the world's most beautiful and esteemed monasteries. Jeff was anticipating a state of tranquillity, but instead he found himself hurtling down a winding mountain road in a mini van singing 'Hey Jude' on the in-car karaoke machine: 'It seems that our driver, who I've dubbed Sensei Rental Car, was a complete psycho whose idea of enlightenment includes the infamous – and long – "Na-na-na" section.' While karaoke may have disrupted Jeff's search for spiritual tranquillity, others were greatly amused by it. When Adrienne McGuire from Alaska spent ten days in South Korea in March 2001, she found karaoke establishments the most amusing places she visited in the country, indeed so amusing she wanted to return to Korea soon:

> My first visit to a Korean karaoke joint was a trip within a trip. My friends and I were shown to a booth with couches and a large screen TV. Once inside we were asked how long we would like to stay (we paid by the half-hour), and the time was set on the screen. We chose from lists of Korean songs, American songs, and Michael Jackson songs. There are several microphones on the table and a tambourine. Drinks were ordered and served. We were to program the selections into the TV as soon as a song was chosen, however all the directions were written in Korean. This is where it was helpful to have been dragged there by a Korean friend (he did all the programming)! At the end of the song the program rated our accuracy. Let's just say none of us scored anywhere near Alanis Morrisette. As we were leaving, we noticed another option available for the more advanced karaoke artists . . . I want to go back to Korea soon.[26]

Jonathan Walsh from Ireland taught English in Korea in 2002 and discovered karaoke as a social lubricant that helped him to mix with the local population:

> A *Noraebang* is a smallish room, not a whole bar. At the front there's a large video screen, with a laser disc player attached and a couple of microphones. Then around the sides there's comfy seating for about twenty people – so you're singing just in front of the people with whom you go in there in the first place . . .

Everyone gets up and sings their song or two. Everyone has a go, and no one is laughed at. The Koreans are super-enthusiastic about such places. You sing a little and soon enough everyone is joining in, shouting back the lyrics if they know them, or making up for any shortage of musical talent with an overflowing enthusiasm to clap, stamp feet or just wave the arms and join in a little dancing. Maybe because I had a little alcohol to lubricate the process, or maybe it was just the effervescent attitude of my hosts, but before long, I was up on the stage air-guitaring to the 'Bohemian Rhapsody'. Much to my surprise I really loved it![27]

It is common for both Koreans and expatriates to crawl to a late-night karaoke club together. Members of the us military, however, are not usually welcomed, since they have a reputation for fighting and making unwanted sexual advances to their female hosts. American soldiers from the nearby us military base at Waogwon, for example, are regularly refused admission to karaoke places in Kumi.[28]

Karaoke is also reported to have helped promote a sense of unity between people of the communist north and those of the capitalist south. On 15 August 2000 a few families from South Korea were permitted to join their northern brethren for a three-day reunion. The event took place on a tour bus equipped with a karaoke machine and over the three days they sang their hearts out. It was claimed that 'songs invigorate spirits and express, refine emotions everywhere, but they do so more to Koreans. Lyrics expressing pathos, filial piety toward long-lost relatives or hopes for the day of reunification are rapidly winning the hearts of people these days.' The number they sang the most was 'Unification is Our Sole Dream'. Its simple yet serene melody was originally composed as a children's song in 1947, when the entire nation was virtually plunged into chaos following its long-awaited liberation from 36 years of Japanese colonial rule in 1945. 'From Seoul to Pyongyang' was another popular song, allegedly composed before 1990 by a taxi driver, who explains: 'I once had an elderly passenger who apparently hailed me to take him to the North. He got in, and said, "Take me to Pyongyang!".' Moved, yet unable to express his feelings, he wrote the song, set to a lively melody:

It costs only 20,000 won to go from Seoul to Pyongyang by taxi. We can go to the Soviet Union, we can go to the moon, we can go anywhere. Why can't we go to Pyongyang, which is closer than Kwangju? . . . And if I don't have passengers on my way back, I will just take along the letters and souls of my brethren who took their pain all the way into death.[29]

Unification is still but a dream.

There is also a darker side. At some Korean karaoke clubs intended for male patronage, clients can rent female entertainers for the evening. Their job is to play the tambourine, sing pop songs, pour men beer, feed them dried squid, clap enthusiastically and pay them non-stop compliments regardless of their atrocious singing. Korean businessmen often take these private singing rooms very seriously. Expensive bottles of whiskey are opened and sometimes more than $1,000 can be spent during a single night: co-workers often compete to pick up the bill to demonstrate their higher status. Important business deals are often hatched between companies as their executives sing through the night. Ken May recalls that many wives often complained to him during their English lessons that their husbands didn't come back from the karaoke clubs until 4.00 am. Compared to many other countries in Asia, however, prostitution in Korean karaoke is still relatively rare.

Karaoke Wonderland: *South-east Asia*

Live by Karaoke: Thailand and Indonesia

If prostitution in karaoke venues is still quite rare in Korea, 'picking up' a girl at a karaoke bar is common practice in South-east Asia. In Thailand, according to a survey produced by the Communicable Disease Control Department in 2001, more than a thousand karaoke establishments employed sex workers. In Indonesia, especially in places like Jakarta and Bali, the first thing one does when entering a karaoke is to choose a girl: usually there is a small window that allows one to see the girls, whereas the girls can only see the client's eyes. Most of these 'hostesses' are very young. Once the choice is made, the girl goes with the client to a private room to 'sing'. Officially the karaoke girls must not be called prostitutes, since prostitution is legally banned in this part of the world. There is, however, an ample supply of sex workers and service girls – including karaoke hostesses. 'Sex tourism' is a major attraction and contributes much to the economy of many South-east Asian countries. The buzzword here is to have 'fun'. Lisa, a 25-year-old working in one of Bali's most famous karaoke venues, testifies that: 'Most guys just want to have fun. Often they touch you or take you in their arms, but that's all. At least inside of karaoke . . . ' Karaoke venues in Bali, indeed, operate under rules that differ from those of brothels: all private rooms have windows and during the working hours security men are employed to ensure 'privacy' at a 'politically correct' level. However what happens after 3 o'clock in the morning, the official closing time for karaoke venues on the island, is considered the private concern of the

girls and their clients. Niluh, a journalist in Bali, says: 'In this country, we must admit that most karaoke venues are a good way for rich men to find girls and take them back home. Some customers do like singing, but sex is part of the game too.' Alain, a French expatriate living in Bali, disagrees; according to him, karaoke venues are places where many girls start their career as prostitutes.[1]

For many Indonesian girls, to work in a karaoke is a 'dream job'. It pays ten times the average salary simply for having 'fun' with customers: in theory, the job only demands that the girls sing, laugh and drink with the clients. The drinks are on the customers and the girls can have as much as they desire. By 3 am the work is over and it's time to go home. The reality, however, may be quite different. According to a report produced by Bill Guerin for *Jakarta Eye*, most girls working in karaoke bars on Batam, a fast-growing estate island close to Singapore, are forced to supply sex to customers, who mainly come from Singapore and Malaysia. Most of these girls are aged between 17 and 30. Clients pay between $10 and $20 a time for intercourse. There are many freelance 'brokers' who supply girls for karaoke bars in return for a commission on each girl they introduce. An attractive girl at a karaoke bar can fetch about $400.[2] Young girls from Bali and Java are also being recruited to perform traditional dances in entertainment centres in Japan, according to a report published by the International Catholic Migration Commission and the American Center for International Labor Solidarity (2003). Once there, however, they are put to work in karaoke bars or strip clubs where they are required to provide sex services to clients.[3]

Similar cases can also be found in Thailand, as a journalist was told by one girl who left Cambodia to seek a new life in Thailand and ended up as a sex worker: 'When I left my country I didn't intend to work here (a karaoke bar). I didn't know this kind of job before. No one told me from the beginning that I would end up in prostitution.'[4] Thailand has become the centre of traffic for karaoke girls. Gangs operate a sophisticated system that covers several countries and supplies the rest of the world. Girls are brought into Thailand not only from Cambodia, but also from Laos, Burma and China (mainly from Yunnan province), and then sent on to Singapore, Japan, the United States and Europe. If the owner of a karaoke bar calls up wanting five service girls, a dealer picks them out at the abandoned shop where they are kept and makes the delivery straightaway; in return he pockets a total of 25,000 baht (about $615).

Rayong, a popular Thai resort south-east of Bangkok with 100 kilometres of coastline, has a port with countless karaoke lounges, outside which women in heavy make-up approach passers-by. Their targets are often migrant workers from Cambodia who have just come ashore after weeks at sea and do not even wait for night to fall before heading out for some 'fun'. Their favourite haunts are karaoke joints – the nearer to the dock, the more convenient – where they gather around a table to drink and, passing the microphone from one to another, sing Khmer melodies and take it in turns to tease the female employees. They may spend about 500 baht (about $12) during a night of karaoke, but the girls get only about 50 baht ($1.2), without meals, and are allowed barely any days off. Owners of karaoke bars insist the girls are there to entertain, not to supply sex to customers, although, according to a report in the *Bangkok Post*, karaoke bars have mushroomed in the Mekong region in recent years, partly due to the sex offered during a night of song.[5] Every evening girls at many of these bars are quickly booked up by customers.

Although some in Thailand are worried about the decline in morals, it would be hard to ban the sex industry completely, since it is a major source of the country's revenue. Instead drastic measures have been taken to protect the youth. For a while, for example, anyone under the age of eighteen was banned from going into a karaoke bar. This only led to a greater diversity of karaoke joints. Now men looking for something more than just a night of song go to 'Adult only Karaoke', leaving everyone else to 'natural' entertainment venues.

A good example of these 'natural' entertainment venues is the SF Music City, which opened just before Christmas 2002 on the top floor of Bangkok's gigantic Mahboonkrong (MBK) shopping centre. Next to the city's biggest movie entertainment complex, SF Music City has 34 karaoke rooms and attracts more than 500 people each weekday and about 700 at the weekend. These are made up of equal numbers of men and women, and most appear to be fairly young. According to Mr Kongpon, its General Manager, 'During daytime, customers are mostly students, aged 17 or 18. At night, the population is slightly older, around 25–26 years old'.[6]

There are more than 5,000 Karaoke venues in Thailand, with more and more 'karaoke booths', charging 10 baht (about 25 cents) for a song, popping up in big department stores. Karaoke is far from over. Thai teenagers and youngsters love to go to karaoke boxes because 'we enjoy being together and singing'. The same can be said elsewhere in South-east Asia for the more family-orientated karaoke boxes. The V-Mix in Hong Kong, for example, is a huge 'karaoke-for-all' facility. It opened in 1999 and claims to be the biggest K-Box (karaoke box) in South-east Asia. Costing $16 million and covering nearly 7,500 square metres, it has 151 rooms and a staff of 150. Some large private rooms can accommodate up to 25 singers. It is open 24 hours a day, 365 days a year, and during public holidays it is often packed with customers from all over South-east Asia, China, Japan and Korea.

To help clean up karaoke's bad image in Bali, in 2003 the Gion Karaoke took out advertisements explaining that it offered two different kinds of karaoke: 'white karaoke', for families or youngsters who just wanted to sing, and 'adult only' (i.e. male-orientated) karaoke for those looking for 'special songs' (or beyond). One of the favourite karaoke destinations for Indonesians on the island is the Diamond, which offers very large rooms, targeting whole families who can even use a well-equipped kitchen while doing karaoke. On the other hand, the nearby Bintang Karaoke, one of the oldest in town, is very popular with Taiwanese, Japanese or Chinese tourists. Karaoke boxes are often the most luxurious places in Bali. In the island's main city, Denpasar, for example, they are probably the only places, besides modern shopping malls, to have lifts, thick carpets and dozens of leather sofas. Karaoke is also cheap in Indonesia, even the most luxurious venues charge less than $15 per hour for the biggest rooms, plus $5 per hour for the escort girl.[7]

Karaoke in Bangkok is twice as expensive, although the city also has plenty of alternative venues offering good value for money. Among these are the 'Auto-Karaoke machines', which are dotted all over the metropolis, from inside big shopping malls to outside public toilets. According to a report in 2002, there were then five thousand Auto-Karaoke machines in Bangkok alone, and seven thousand countrywide. These dimly lit automated booths come in various sizes catering for groups of between two and six persons. Fitted with doors, they are sound-proofed to provide privacy for users. For just 10 baht, people can enjoy the intimacy of being of packed like sardines and sing. Each booth is equipped with a video monitor, speakers and microphones. There is no cover charge, no drinks to pay for and no hostess to tip. Customers can use the booth as long as they like. Teenagers love them: 'It is a good form of amusement for me and my friends when we hang out at the weekends . . . It is cheaper than watching movies or sitting in the coffee houses, and here we can dance too.' They are particularly popular with couples, although entire families have been seen squeezing inside one box. Business is brisk at the weekends. Indeed, the demand is so high that on average booth operators such as Uraipan Sae-Lor can break even after six months and start to make a profit. Ms

Uraipan, who owns seventeen booths in the Central Shopping Centre in Bangkok, said each machine cost her 70,000 baht ($2,950), 'but I have already recovered my investments'.[8]

With the advance of technology, doing karaoke is getting cheaper and easier. In most of South-east Asia nowadays it's hard to buy a CD player that does not include the K-function (karaoke function). In Thailand there are numerous websites offering an 'online karaoke virtual experience', the pioneer in the field being www.singingweb.com, which is available in English and Thai. For some years manufacturers in Thailand have sought to rival Japan's place at the forefront of the karaoke business; this has made some Thais inventive.

On 12 May 2003 the *Bangkok Post* reported that Vichian Simma, a 23-year-old from north-eastern Buriram, had allegedly created the world's first 'karaoke taxi'. 'I like music very much and every time I drove past a karaoke bar I thought of it,' says Simma. Tired of the loneliness and silence of driving a rented taxi, Simma took out a loan, bought his own cab and installed karaoke equipment. The set consists of a mini-television near the front passenger seat, two microphones and a video player. In addition, there's a set of flashing lights to recreate that groovy disco atmosphere even in the heaviest of traffic. There is a selection of twenty videos ranging from classics to pop hits. Songs are mostly in Thai, English or Japanese, with Thai love songs being the most popular. The idea was an immediate hit and passengers flocked to him, as one passenger explained: 'I feel happy when using this taxi. The karaoke taxi gives me a chance to forget about heavy traffic and to relax while waiting.' Speaking to the *Bangkok Post*, Simma said: 'Some can't get enough, especially if they've just left the bar. Others tell me to drive around for a bit more just so they can sing.' Occasionally Simma even shares his passion for singing and joins customers for a karaoke. There is no extra charge for using the karaoke facilities. With his newly installed karaoke equipment, Simma's business has increased sharply. By the time of the report, he was earning more than 20,000 baht ($470) a month, and his tips had risen dramatically.[9] In 2004 Simma added internet service into his taxi, so his passengers can surf the web for a wider choice of karaoke songs.[10]

Overleaf: in Bangkok, Thailand.

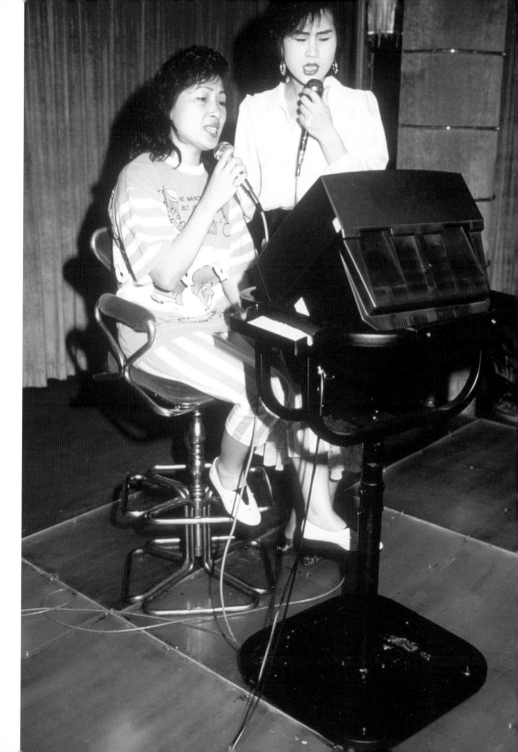

Now that karaoke taxis are no longer a novelty they can be seen in many of Asia's major cities, from Singapore to Taipei and Shanghai. A taxi driver in Singapore even boasted that the karaoke machine released his stress. After they became used to riding in the karaoke taxi, Thais began to buy karaoke cellphones. These handsets allow people to croon even on the crowded train to work, perhaps with one giving a rendition of Joe Transvestite's 'I feel like a woman', while the person in the next seat is singing 'I feel like an aspirin'.

Karaoke is now such an integral part of everyday life for people in Thailand, with karaoke bars found on every street in every major city, that even the quieter and more sedate northern city of Chiang Mai is crowded with karaoke lounges. Here the favourite haunts for karaoke fans are those located in Chiang Mai Land, a purpose-built street in the southern part of the city just off Changklan Road. Most of these karaoke lounges employ plenty of attractive young hostesses to sit and sing with the customers for a small hourly fee.

'Do it all with your cell phone'

Man: Hi honey. I'm at the grocery store. I'm not sure which ice cream to buy.

Wife: Don't worry, sweetie. I'll help you. Just send me photos of all the choices. And don't forget a close-up of the nutrition facts.

Man: Hang on, honey. I have to stand in line behind 30 other clueless men.

Wife: Really? Well, why don't you entertain them with some karaoke?[11]

Many restaurants are also equipped with sing-along machines so that aspiring singers and inspired amateurs can play to an audience or impress their friends. Even if some sing badly they enjoy it just as well – it's so relaxing and fun. Karaoke bars are known to be a popular dating venue where singles can have a wonderful time and meet new friends. Bangkok is also a city with a lively gay and lesbian scene, and K-Boxes for gays or lesbians can be seen all over. One of the first such establishments was Pharaoh's Music Bar, situated in Silom Soi 4 at the heart of Bangkok's nightlife quarter. It claims to be the city's favourite karaoke bar and features dual karaoke lounges with an extensive list of songs.

As in Korea, singing is an essential part of the everyday life of many ordinary Thais. Whether formal or casual, sacred or mundane, no gathering is complete without some kind of musical performance or spontaneous sing-along. Even if the occasion is just a group of friends hanging out in a park or on a beach, somebody will have a guitar and everybody else forms a chorus. One of Thailand's most important festivals, the Phi Ta Khon Festival in Loei Province, is also a real sing-along fiesta, with musicians from the Issan area playing while everyone else gets up to dance and sing. Situated in north-east Thailand on the border with Laos, the Issan area is famous for Morlam songs. *Mor* means a person of extraordinary abilities, and *Lam* means 'epic song'. Morlam was originally a traditional narrative performance. Most of the population in Issan are of Lao descent, and differ culturally from those of Bangkok and the rest of central Thailand. Morlam performance, as is often claimed, has been used as a social force in Thailand to unite the people of Issan. The lyrics regularly tell the singers' own stories, making reference to village life, their families and loved ones, as well as to the cultural exploitation they experienced in Thailand and elsewhere. In Bangkok Morlam performances are usually held outdoors. The lyrics are sung in the Issan dialect and those in the audience who originally came from Issan to work in the modern metropolis respond in the same. As the music takes its hold, they often increasingly begin to feel 'back home'. Non-Issan people are often attracted by the performance and enjoy themselves in their own way, even though they don't understand the lyrics.[12]

Morlam songs were traditionally sung accompanied by a single *khaen*, a mouth organ made of bamboo. In the course of the twentieth century Morlam developed into a popular singing style, with a certain affinity to both Luk thung (literally 'Country Kid') songs, another form of popular music in Thailand, as well as to Western music. Today the popular Morlam songs are mainly produced in Bangkok and are rarely heard in the Issan region. Entrepreneurs saw the popularity of Morlam songs as a profit-making opportunity and began to market them on CDs. People who had been impressed by the music were often disappointed when listening to them at home, shorn of the proper atmosphere. Karaoke bars, however, can do something to redeem such shortcomings, and for a few baht customers can play a VCD of their favourite Morlam performer. Karaoke bars quickly became ideal locations for the hundreds of thousands of Morlam fans who cannot afford television. Karaoke bars, often equipped with widescreen TVs and the latest technology, allow them to experience their favourite stars on stage, at a venue close to work or home. Many hostesses working in these karaoke bars are also of Issan origin and have ventured into the Thai capital for economic reasons. Their presence often adds to the atmosphere when a Morlam VCD is playing, as they spontaneously get up and dance, turning the place into a wild party.

Today there are special nightclubs in Bangkok featuring live Morlam music seven nights a week, such as Tawan Daeng ('Red Hot Sun' in the Issan language), where popular Morlam stars like Jintara Poonlarb and Monthong Sihavong, whose karaoke VCDs are now widely available, often perform. As well as circulating in Thailand, these VCDs have also been introduced to the West by Morlam enthusiasts such as Geoff Alexander, an archivist and historian from California.

Unlike Morlam, Luk thung does not have a country folk origin, although the term 'Country Kid' suggests the music is about farmers. Luk thung first emerged in Bangkok in the 1950s and its popularity spread to other urban areas in the late 1980s during the Thai economic boom. Luk thung is said to be a uniquely Thai sound, borrowing from an eclectic range of influences including Thai folk and court music, jazz, Latin American music, rock and rap. Since the 1990s there has been much cross-fertilization between Luk thung and Morlam, giving rise to Morlam-inspired Luk thung, such as Luk thung Issan and Luk thung Prayuk. Many Morlam stars also perform Luk thung songs. The backing for Luk thung songs is usually a Western-style band, but the tones and musical embellishments are typically Thai. Most of the lyrics are vivid tales of the everyday life of people who live in the countryside or have left their rural communities to work in the city. For many people, the lyrics of Luk thung are the reality of their lives.[13] As with Morlam songs, you can now get Luk thung karaoke VCDs, although, confusingly, these are sometimes known as Issan karaoke. There is also a website giving instructions how to perform Luk thung karaoke.[14]

Cover of a Morlam karaoke VCD.

Given the glamour that Morlam and Luk thung superstars have bestowed on Thai karaoke, nearby Indonesia does not want to fall behind: one of the high points of the 2004 presidential election campaign was a karaoke duet between two former generals on Indonesia's version of 'Pop Idol'. General Wiranto, the former Commander-in-Chief of the Indonesian armed forces, is a passionate lover of karaoke singing and has spent hundreds of dollars on voice coaching. He has even released a CD of love songs entitled *For you my Indonesia*, including his famous rendition of 'Feeling'. To help clear his blood-stained military record, he even donated the profits from his CD to helping Indonesian refugees. He clearly saw singing as his route to victory. In his commander-in-chief style, he called for an A chord.

As the keyboard players at his side struck up the ballad 'Indonesia is my fatherland – an eternal, glorious treasure', Wiranto sang into the microphone with 'his hips gyrating and arms waving'. The crowd roared its delight. He then held the microphone out to the audience so they could sing the chorus, and he bent down to sweep his palm along a line of outstretched hands – the true style of a star. The mostly 20-something group closest to the stage 'cheered itself hoarse as he concluded his second song', but as he went for a third the sky suddenly opened and a tropical downpour cleared the stadium.[15]

The deluge washed out Wiranto's dream of victory. It turned out that Susilo Bambang Yudhoyono had a better voice, as well as a 'cleaner' record, and he certainly looked good on TV. At the polls he beat Wiranto to become Indonesia's first elected president.

Wiranto the karaoke star.

Karaoke was crucial in the 2004 presidential election. Yet while Wiranto lost, his karaoke legacy lives on, since karaoke helped to make a military dictator look almost human and charming, and provided him with an opportunity to be seen supporting charities. Wiranto, however, is certainly not the only genius to think of supporting charity through karaoke. Resource Development International-Cambodia (RDI) is a private, US-registered, non-profit-making organization that seeks to help the people of Cambodia through various technological and educational projects, and one of these is based on the production of karaoke teaching aids.

Rebirth with karaoke: Cambodia

In its mission statement, RDI Cambodia claims that 'Karaoke is without doubt an effective way of communicating . . . It can and does teach valuable and important information'. It also states that karaoke is the most popular form of entertainment in all of Cambodia: 'In Cambodia virtually everyone likes to participate. Entire families sing along in their homes. Karaoke is sung at large celebrations and parties, small restaurants, and even in outdoor parks. It also does NOT require an audience. Also, every age group participates with equal enthusiasm.'

To make karaoke an effective educational tool, RDI Cambodia has hired Khmer staff, including singers and songwriters, to produce 'uplifting' educational songs for mass distribution in the market and on television. The songs, based on subjects ranging from rice to arsenic, are crafted with lyrics and in styles that most Cambodians would enjoy singing, and the singers and musicians chosen for the vocals and backings of the initial recordings are mostly well known in the country. According to the project leader:

> While Americans might find an educational song to be 'cheesy' or less than desirable, RDI has found that audiences are eager to sing our educational songs . . . Adults and children actually will pick up a microphone and begin singing brand new songs they have never heard before because of the familiar way the songs are produced. In numerous field tests Cambodians are excited to sing along with no prompting. This is truly a culturally appropriate method of combining education with popular entertainment.[16]

To reach the rural population, RDI also has a special karaoke truck, often attracting sizeable crowds in villages and the countryside. Whenever the truck starts to play a karaoke VCD, children clap and sing along, while villagers clamour for the microphone. Often the villagers have learnt a new song or more by the time the truck leaves; most of all, they have memorized the information in the songs. Days later, when the karaoke truck returns to the village, the staff often discover that some villagers have already acted on the instructions given in the songs.[17]

While some might challenge RDI Cambodia for exaggerating the impact of karaoke in Cambodia, it is undeniable that karaoke is really big in the country, so big that in 2001 Prime Minister Hun Sen tried to wipe out karaoke bars owing to their links with prostitution and drug problems. Like any means of combating drugs or prostitution, banning karaoke is a form of social control. When people gather together and enjoy themselves, it is frequently seen as a threat to any totalitarian regime. Too much fun might corrupt the society, thus karaoke becomes the 'enemy within' and must be uprooted.

Since the ban was imposed, karaoke bars have scratched out the word 'karaoke' from their signs and many places have re-emerged as restaurants, canteens and eating houses. Karaoke continued to thrive, however, even after the government confiscated television sets from all public venues and from people's homes. Everywhere the locals have turned karaoke into a live performance. With a synthesizer playing in the background and

In a karaoke club
in Siem Reap,
Cambodia. These
establishments
are now illegal.

Karaoke restaurant that features beer girls and prostitutes. Phnom Penh, Cambodia.

someone leading the singing up front, people get up to sing from the printed lyrics held in their hand. To make friends in Cambodia, all one needs to do is to sing – in return one gets free beer, free food and even a 'No Problem' from the police.[18] With people cheering for karaoke sing-along, musicologists have lamented the gradual loss of traditional Cambodian music following the flood of karaoke tapes across the entire country.[19] Tradition, however, always changes over the course of time, from country to country and culture to culture. Karaoke has in many cases been a means of perpetuating tradition. One good example is the popularity of Mon karaoke in Burma, which has generated much interest in reviving the dying Mon culture and language.

'Karaoke fascism': Burma

Mon is one of the oldest cultures in South-east Asia and is said to be under threat of extinction. Situated in south-eastern Burma, the region was granted statehood by Burma's socialist government in the 1970s. The majority of people living in the 'Mon land', however, now speak Burmese and go to Burmese schools. Until a few years ago young people showed hardly any interest in their Mon cultural heritage, but things began to change in the late 1990s, owing to the efforts of Mon patriots and a number of popular singers of Mon origin interested in reviving the language and culture. Hong Chan's big hit song 'Chan Mon, Chan Nai', sung entirely in the Mon language, is laden with nationalist sentiments. The song was soon made into a VCD and Mon people all over the world have learnt to sing it by doing karaoke. After its initial sales success in 2000, the production company, Mon VCD Karaoke Video & Tape Production, began the search for further titles to follow it. In the following year the company produced six more karaoke VCDs in the Mon language with the intention of replacing all the VCDs in other languages available in the region. The company was backed by the National Musician Organization, which boasted that 'our community faithfully accept them and we can bar our Mon community from singing other languages on VCD karaoke'.[20]

Our own karaoke:
Burmese enjoying
their own karaoke
band.

Most songs in Mon VCD karaoke are in a modern style but accompanied on traditional Mon instruments, often with a contemporary twist that is thought more relevant to contemporary audiences. Some of the songs are translated Burmese pop songs, and others are translated from Thai and English. Before the VCDs may be sold, however, permission must be granted by the Military Government Censorship Department in Burma, which will not allow Mon singers to produce songs unless the covers and song titles are also translated into Burmese.

The young people who pack karaoke bars in 'Mon land' often meet visitors from the outside world. Young Thais and Burmese are frequent patrons and their love of Mon karaoke has led them to a deeper interest in the Mon culture. Mon karaoke has also spread as far as Europe: a Mon National Day Celebration held in Utrecht, Netherlands, on 27 February 2005 offered 'traditional Mon karaoke', as well as typical Mon food, as an example of the Mon cultural heritage.

Indeed, for the Mon people and others in Myanmar (Burma), karaoke is as essential as rice. The title of Monique Skidmore's book *Karaoke Fascism: Burma and Politics of Fear* (2004) is an apt metaphor capturing the importance of karaoke in everyday life in this part of the world – especially as a means of escape from poverty, fear and fascist oppression. Karaoke has also become an important part of the local economy, a situation in which the United States is thought to have played an unwitting role.

In 1997 the Clinton administration first imposed sanctions on Burma. Six years later, the US Congress overwhelmingly approved more rigorous sanctions by passing the Burmese Freedom and Democracy Act, which banned all Burmese imports for one year. In 2004 President Bush extended the act for a further year. The sanctions hurt the Rangoon regime financially, resulting in the closure of many garment factories. It was reported that more than 80,000 textile workers lost their jobs. For many, karaoke bars became their only means of making a livelihood. Min Min, a young girl working in a well-known karaoke bar in downtown Rangoon, for example, earns a basic wage of about 50,000 kyat ($55) a month, nearly double her pay when she worked in a Rangoon garment factory. Min Min went to work in the karaoke bar as a means of saving herself from poverty and perhaps becoming a famous singer, although the reality is somehow different. 'It's like working in a brothel. Most customers caress me. If I refuse, they will find another girl', she told a reporter. Dependent on the money – much of which goes to supporting her family – she has no way out. To make enough, some girls have to work in several bars. Exclusive karaoke bars in Rangoon are often full of high-ranking government officials and rich businessmen. To survive in the business, bar owners regularly invite officials in for some 'relaxation'.[21] It seems no one here can live without karaoke. Karaoke makes the world of Rangoon go around.

In early 2005, on-site karaoke venues were even being built at the new Myanmar National Convention. Delegates were expected to have a grand karaoke time away from the world, although the opposition parties and ordinary people, who were denied the opportunity of attending the Convention, had nothing to sing about.[22]

'We rule Karaoke': the Philippines

While privileged delegates in Burma have been provided with the luxury to enjoy their karaoke away from the rest of world, the outcasts in Philippine prisons are denied the pleasure of their favourite pastime – in 2005 the Philippine government banned karaoke nights in all prisons to save electricity. To deny a Filipino the right of enjoying karaoke is like stopping a person's heart beating. To many Filipinos, karaoke is so fundamental to their life that owning a karaoke machine is far more important than having a toilet in their home. Most people in Manila live in very cramped accommodation. Often the whole family is squeezed into one room and it is common for ten families to share a toilet. Most homes have hardly anything apart from a few mattresses. A karaoke machine, however, is almost always in sight – singing to their hearts' content is the only way many Filipinos have to relieve life's misery.

If karaoke is Korea's national sport, for Filipinos karaoke is their national pride. As Rich Kiamco, a well-known American-Filipino writer and performing artist, once said: 'The Japanese might have invented karaoke, but the Filipinos RULE it!' While many Asians might find this statement highly debatable, the majority of Filipinos really believe they have the best pipes and will prove it by hogging the microphone for the rest of the night and belting 'Wind beneath my Wings' with melodramatic fervour.[23] When Enter Tech (ET) Corporation, a leading Korean home entertainment company that had a huge success with its 'Magic Sing Along' Compact Microphone (known as the Magic Sing Mic), recently chose the Philippines as its latest investment hub, President Gloria Macapagal-Arroyo told the Korean investors: 'Thank you for choosing the Philippines. The Filipinos love to sing and 90 per cent of the Filipinos sing well.'

With karaoke being the country's premier pastime, the Department of Tourism and In-A-Jiffy Enterprise (ET's subsidiary in the Philippines) have come up with the brilliant idea of combining karaoke with promoting tourism through the fabulous 'Sing with the Philippines' Magic Singing Package, which comprises famous scenes in the Philippines that have been immortalized in song accompanied by the appropriate video footage.

Whether 'Sing with the Philippines' has boosted the country's tourism or not is another matter. There is, however, hardly any doubt that the Magic Sing Mic was an enormous hit in the Philippines. The country's most controversial movie actress, Kris Aquino, even wrote in her weekly *Philippine Star* column how the Magic Sing Mic kept her up all night with endless singing enjoyment.[24] Ms Aquino was certainly not seen as controversial this time. She was, in fact, in good company, since Manila is famous for being a twenty-four-hour karaoke city, and no night and no celebration is complete in the Philippines without karaoke singing.

In the Philippines there are millions of karaoke machines, all apparently loaded with the Sinatra classics that been an integral part of the long nights of so many Filipinos over the last 40 years. Frank brought much joy to the people of the Philippines. In Manila, known as 'drinkers' paradise', whenever the drink starts to flow and the karaoke is turned on, it is certain that 'My Way' won't be far away. Manila is also a city full of guys who look just like Frank Sinatra; Ted Lerner, an American-born travel writer who has lived in the Philippines and other parts of Asia, once described Manila as 'the perfect Sinatra kind of town':

> Sinatra with the quasi-mob connections and the persona of the charming street thug. That's a near perfect description of the kind of people you often meet in Manila. They are guys who could well be called Mr Hospitality, Mr Action, Mr Excitement. In Manila you always see guys snapping their fingers to call somebody's attention to do something for them. Even the language comes from the Al Capone era. People call each other 'boss'. Congressmen and senators are referred to as 'solons' . . . Manila's a city that has thousands of little fiefdoms, subject to dudes who run their own program in some corner of a little neighbourhood with a dozen or so loyal associates and hangers-on. Lord knows what these guys did on a daily basis. But whatever program they were running, nobody messed with it. Charming wheeler dealers, big shots, guys who like to spread cash, gamblers, wise guys, big bosses, punks and partiers all in a 24 hour town where you can get anything you want – and don't want – whenever you want it. That's Manila, a city that's got everything people associate with the Frank Sinatra persona, all played out openly.[25]

'All played out openly': people in Manila certainly love doing karaoke openly. Never mind the private Japanese karaoke boxes, for the Filipinos doing karaoke openly is 'My Way' and the only way – even the so-called 'private karaoke clubs' are open-style in the Philippines. From huge Chinese

'Star in a million' show.

restaurants to noisy drinking houses, public parks and the crowded quarters where most people live, with the help of the portable and affordable Magic Sing Mic, karaoke makes the sound of Manila. While everyone is totally immersed in 'My Way', no one seems bothered about others screaming down the microphone, even if the noise is ear-splitting and appetite-squelching. Oliver Coultrup, a student from Southampton who worked as a volunteer in the Philippines, noted karaoke's incredible popularity, no matter how bad the singer: 'The last time I was in a mall a girl was not disheartened even though she was mercilessly butchering a song in front of thousands of people. Slushy ballads are all winners here; they love them like a fat kid loves cake.'[26]

In Manila, karaoke is more than just singing: it is a shared experience about everyday living. The Filipinos are proud, dramatic, defiant, emotional, yet tolerant and forgiving, and 'My Way' is their perfect song: 'I've had my fill, my share of losing . . . And now . . . as tears subside . . . I find it all, so amusing . . . '

Filipinos like to regard themselves as karaoke kings and queens, and almost everyone wants to get onto one of the many popular 'Star' shows, the country's versions of the 'Pop Idol' format, from 'Star in a Million' and 'Star Circle Quest' to 'Star Struck'. According to data from AGB Philippines, more than two million TV viewers are hooked on each of the shows, rising to more than six million on the grand final nights. In modern society where time is money and 'instant' reigns, from instant coffee to instant cash, variety 'Star' shows in the Philippines produce instant celebrities.

It is thought that in everyone there lurks a latent 'diva'. That is what makes people hog the microphone and fall for karaoke. The millions in the Philippines who cannot enter the television variety shows, however, can now cut their own album thanks to Nescafé. To attract consumers and build up an image as a youth brand, the Nestlé Company held a 'Coffee Personalities' contest among Philippine university students. For the competition, karaoke bars were built shaped like giant Nescafé jars, where people could sing along with their favourite tunes and have their recorded efforts burned onto a CD.

Karaoke therapy: Singapore

Nescafé 3-in-1 (with sugar and Coffeemate, a popular mixture) and karaoke are the two great passions of many of the fashionable young in South-east Asia, where there is a widespread cultural preference for all things packaged – from food to music. In a fast-changing modern society full of uncertainty, packaging provides a sense of security and familiarity. This might explain the incredible appeal of ready-made sugary milky coffee and ready-chosen syrupy karaoke pops. For many Singaporean students living in London, the two things that make them feel homesick are when they cannot do karaoke 'properly' and cannot indulge in super-sweet creamy instant 3-in-1 Nescafé.

In Singapore both karaoke and Nescafé are so big that the streets are covered with advertising billboards proclaiming the likes of 'Wellness in your life, Nestlé in your life', 'If you are looking for a Caribbean tune, learn Jimmy Cliff's "I can see clearly now the rain has gone"' and 'Karaoke Class at Community Centre'. While the Nestlé Company in Singapore promises 'Good Life, Good Food', karaoke singing has been incorporated into social and health programmes by various community centres and religious organizations. The Diocese of Singapore, for example, joined up with the Institute of Mental Health in Singapore to operate a Karaoke Happy Hour session for all its unemployed members on Mondays to Fridays from 5 to 6 pm. The Diocese encourages all of its members to work towards building a healthy body and mind. As well as kicking the bad habit of smoking and doing fitness workouts, it is suggested that during the Karaoke Happy Hours 'everyone learns to unwind by listening to music, dancing, and singing, making a joyful noise to the Lord'. Some mental health experts even proposed using karaoke therapy in the rehabilitation of mental patients.

In 2002 a certain Ms Ng Wang Feng sent a letter to the editor of the *Singapore Medical Journal* stating that 'Karaoke may be beneficial to patients as described by having positive effects on self-esteem, social skills training and social phobia.' That December the journal published an article by Dr Arthur Dun-Ping Mak and Dr C. M. Leong of the Department of Psychiatry at the Prince of Wales Hospital and the Chinese University of

Hong Kong, which argues that the use of karaoke as a form of music therapy in treating mental patients has a number of advantages:

> In a practical sense, conducting proper karaoke sessions as it is commonly experienced requires less training on the part of the therapist, such that it can be administrated by any medical or paramedical staff. At the same time, being fashionable, karaoke is a welcome activity among most local mental patients. It is thought that karaoke, under social circumstances of friendly gatherings, places the participant in a uniquely active role in music perception and performance. In contrast to other common local listening activities where music is cast more in the background than the forefront, I argue that karaoke provides a unique opportunity where the common local citizen is placed in the closest and most autonomous relationship to music as it is performed.
>
> It is also observed that participants of karaoke are less likely to be affected by social anxiety compared to other forms of music performance, and usually express their feelings more easily. From a theoretical standpoint, the experience of karaoke echoes psychodynamic processes that have been observed in music therapy sessions, in that the participants identify themselves variously with characters and moods pictured and described in the songs they perform, and conversely may project their own feelings onto songs they perform, thus expressing their feelings in their performance.[27]

Since 1990 the Department of Psychiatry at the Prince of Wales Hospital in Hong Kong has been using karaoke as a therapy in treating mental patients. According to Dr Mak, the combination of images and singing has helped people to focus on positive thoughts. Furthermore, he says, 'karaoke tends to bolster self image, decrease stage anxiety and encourage social interactions.'

'New change,' new life with karaoke: Vietnam

Karaoke's contributions to mental well-being are also believed to play a positive role in learning languages. A shining example of this is provided by English-language teaching in Vietnam. Since the implementation of the Doi Moi ('new change') policy by the Vietnamese government in 1986, learning English has become very popular for young Vietnamese, especially from secondary school onwards. A flood of EFL teachers from Australia, New Zealand, the United Kingdom and the United States has been recruited into the country. The popularity of karaoke in Vietnam, plus the locals' fondness for singing and Western songs, has led many language teachers and schools to use karaoke in teaching, as one teacher explained:

> Karaoke is very useful in teaching English. We like it as we can listen to the song and read the words at the same time. We also learn many interesting words from different songs. When I just listened to a song, I didn't understand, but the words on the screen helped a lot. Karaoke is very popular in Vietnam, but we must make use of it in language teaching in classes.[28]

Mark Huy Lê, a researcher at the University of Tasmania, conducted fieldwork on the role of music in language teaching in Vietnam. Among the people Mark interviewed, one claimed that 'I like Western music. Sometimes I don't understand exactly what a song is about, but somehow I could feel the message.' Another went on to state that 'music brings people together. I enjoy listening to classical music. I don't need to go to Paris or New York. I just sit at this cafe and the music can bring me somewhere in the world.'[29]

Music and singing make up an essential part of everyday life and education for Vietnamese youth. From as early as primary school, children learn to sing songs about their duties to their families, friends and country, and songs about the war. Patriotism and war are still the main themes in the Vietnamese music repertory, including some of the most popular karaoke songs. There are also love songs dedicated to the country, such as those composed by Trinh Cong Son, who has sometimes been hailed as the 'Bob Dylan of Vietnam'. Son was born in 1939 and grew up to witness his beloved country being torn apart by wars and invasions. Fuelled by nostalgia and love for his country, many of Son's songs portray the horror of the war and criticize the decadence of Saigon society. Although his work is not rigidly ideological or political (he did not sing, for example, about the heroic battles for the liberation of the Vietnamese people), after his death in 2001 he was enthroned as a national hero and his songs are often sung with fervent patriotism. In most Vietnamese karaoke, both in Vietnam and abroad, Son's 'Diem Xua' (My Nostalgia) has become the most popular choice. It is rather ironic that, although Son's songs are mostly very calm and peaceful, many Vietnamese prefer to listen to them in crowded and noisy karaoke bars with their friends and buddies.

While Son's songs have become an expression of Vietnamese love for their country, the Co people of central and northern Vietnam also use music to stir up feelings of patriotism and fighting spirit as they campaign for national freedom. The Co inhabit the Tra Bong district in Quang Ngai province in central Vietnam and the Tra My district in the Quang Nam province in northern Vietnam. They are known for having a song for literally everything, from love to daily activities. As an oppressed ethnic group, music has played an important role in the Co's struggle for freedom, as Truong Ngoc Khang, a local Co official, explained to Jan Dodd, the author of *The Rough Guide to Vietnam*: 'In order to organize an uprising in Tra Bong District and Western Quang Ngai Province we took many tunes from different ethnic groups like the Co, H're and the Ca doong to stir up patriotism.' Most young Co, however, do not know these songs and they survive only in the memories of the elderly. With the help of local patriots, they have now been preserved on CDs and VCDs, and can always be found in karaoke bars.

As a patriotic tool, karaoke has the power to unite. It also has the ability to enhance social harmony and preserve lost traditions. In Vietnam, as in other parts of Asia, karaoke often becomes the place where the old meets the young, tradition meets modernity: when all the generations of the family sit together in front of the karaoke machine to sing and share their love and nostalgia, lost music is often revived through this modern media. Karaoke, however, can also bring changes, corrupt old values and destabilize society. Towards the end of the 1990s, as it began to open up to the Western world, sweeping changes took place in Vietnam. One noticeable example was that VTV, one of the state television channels, began to air a lunchtime programme teaching people to sing karaoke, including songs by many Western artists. Excerpts from MTV were also screened, showing videos with lyrics and images that were far more provocative than the Vietnamese cultural commissars allowed for domestic musicians.[30]

As the old Saigon returns to life, everything 'Western' has suddenly seemed innately superior, from Coca-Cola to Western songs. Almost overnight the Americans, the old enemy, have become great friends, and walking into any *pho* shop one can always find western rock videos blaring from a TV and a VCR. From 'Band on the Run' to a Vietnamese torch song filmed in Orange County, California, diners can enjoy a virtual and musical experience of Americana while downing their bowl of noodle soup, or settling comfortably down on a traditional style lacquer settee.[31] Although Western pop songs are enthusiastically accepted by young Vietnamese, they seem to care little for the cultural meanings associated with these songs. With their stress on individual freedom, sexual liberation and social hostility, the messages of Western pop songs oppose those qualities that

Karaoke during a wedding banquet, Ho Chi Minh City, Vietnam.

Vietnamese most treasure: serenity, love, care and sharing. In adapting Western songs to the Vietnamese cultural context, visual images shown on VCDs made for the Vietnamese market, most of which are produced in Hong Kong, France and Southern California, are generally peaceful scenes, such as neon-green rice fields, jagged mountains and rock-strewn harbours, similar to those promoted by the local tourist board as appropriate to the 'Vietnamese sensibility'.[32]

The Vietnamese are a romantic people, and their passion for karaoke has a romantic flavour. Among the hundreds of karaoke bars in Saigon, there are even a number of romantic floating karaoke boats on the Saigon River. The most prominent, and perhaps the biggest, of these is situated close to the renowned Floating Hotel. Every evening, after nightfall, young couples ride together on their little scooters to find their favourite karaoke place, where they sing love duets together. Most of these karaoke bars are just a tiny, simply decorated room, often next door to the room where the owner lives. They are also cheap: one dollar pays for half an hour's hire, plus chocolate cookies and other Western snacks.

'Serious karaoke' on a boat, Vietnam.

Of course, like everywhere else, there are many types of karaoke in Vietnam, including the more infamous. Here these are known as 'Bia Om', which literally means 'beer and a hug', or 'Karaoke Om' ('holding karaoke'), since men, including large numbers of Westerners and Japanese, can hold the hands of the karaoke girls, also known as 'fun girls', while singing. A typical 'Bia Om' has private rooms where a group of buddies can sit on a couch in front of a big screen TV warbling their favourite hits and oldies. In addition to a case of beer next to them on the floor, each man often has a hostess to help him 'ease a tune along'.

Catching up with many of its neighbouring countries, sex tourism in Vietnam is increasing daily. Out of a population of six million, Saigon has, according to an official report, more than 15,000 prostitutes. While street-walkers are seen patrolling outside churches, the city is full of establishments ranging from 'Hot Toc Om' ('hair cut and a hug') to 'Bida Om' ('billiards and a hug'). Together they keep men in Saigon very busy indeed. Striptease and peep shows cannot be found in Vietnam, however, since it is considered completely bizarre to watch without touching, while phone sex is thought a perversion.

Karaoke at a FELDA wedding, Johor, Malaysia. Here a karaoke session is one of the wedding entertainments. Karaoke providers usually include a DJ and several singers. At the same time, guests are invited to sing. Usually this will last throughout the wedding, from 10 am to 5 pm.

Beyond the Gospel

While sex tourism is a fast-growing industry in South-east Asia, karaoke is spreading even more rapidly. Within a few years it has even infiltrated its way to people generally considered as still untouched by the Christian Gospel. One good example is the Aeta people in the northern Philippines. While the Southeast Asia Mission Team, an evangelical Christian organization, regards the Aeta people as still awaiting evangelization, karaoke has gone ahead of the missionaries and captured those survivors hidden in the jungle. When a representative of Peoples of the World, an organization working with indigenous groups around the world, visited the Aeta living on the island of Luzon, he was surprised to find that one of the duties of the headman in one Aeta village was to look after the village's karaoke machine. Every evening children flocked in front of the Magic Sing Mic to give their rendition of Western songs.

The Moken, known as the sea gypsies, have been sailing across the Andaman Sea for centuries, living as nomadic boat dwellers scattered among the 800 islands of the Mergui archipelago. They are animists, with a unique culture, language and way of living that makes them ethnically quite separate from the people of Thailand or Myanmar. In the aftermath of the 2005 tsunami catastrophe, two hundred Moken were among the few survivors who continued to live on the islands of the Ko Surin National Marine Park in Phang Nga district, on the west coast of Thailand. To help rebuild their lives, karaoke machines, televisions and DVD players have been introduced into the Moken villages. It will probably not be long before tourists flock back and join these sea gypsies for a night of wild karaoke!

The Disneyland of
Karaoke Palaces: *China*

According to the *World Press Review*, karaoke is now officially out of fashion in China: 'In the early 1990s karaoke bars were all the rage in Beijing. But now many karaoke clubs are struggling to survive. In fact, 800 karaoke halls in Beijing have already closed down.' The reason for this, says Guan Tiehan of the Beijing Culture Administration, is that 'Beijing is very fad conscious' and 'karaoke has passed its prime. It seems that Beijingers are finding that watching their friends sing badly just isn't worth it.'[1]

But in reality it is not karaoke that is 'out'. In China today, only those who think of KTV (Karaoke Television) as merely an entertainment are completely 'out'. KTV is an integral part of human and cultural experience in contemporary China: it is so 'out' that it's 'in'! While a few pretentious, middle-class, urban professionals go to Starbucks, real people go to karaoke. It can be dirt cheap and there are discounted rates in the early morning, early evening and in off-peak hours during the day. Time passes by quickly at karaoke. Watching the sunrise when one leaves KTV makes life seem as beautiful as it really should be.

Melody is the hottest karaoke joint in the imperial capital, Beijing: to claim a place after 9 pm you have to book a day in advance. Melody has a 'clean' reputation. 'Clean' in contemporary China can mean many things, but here it means you can have a fun night out with friends without paying a huge amount for extra services, or buying drinks for 'service girls'. Melody is a massive building just outside of the second ring road. With its substantial presence of migrant white-collar professionals and poor

Students at Melody karaoke bar, Beijing, China.

workers, as well a huge number of Russians, the area has been nicknamed 'foreigners street' (*laofan jie*). Every night at Melody there are hordes of people sitting at café tables, drinking beer and waiting for the next karaoke room to empty. Offering an extensive selection of Chinese and English songs, it's a popular venue with both Chinese and foreigners. People go there to sing, to have birthday parties or a night out with their colleagues – even if you can't get a place to sing, it's just as fun to sit in the waiting hall, watch the crowds, chat with mates and drink cheap beer.

Melody might be great fun, but it's nothing like New Chinatown (*Tangren jie*), the Disneyland of karaoke palaces. As China is turning into the world's biggest Disneyland, a visit to New Chinatown becomes a quintessential Chinese experience. This huge theme park has a main street with mock Tang dynasty façades, leaving you wondering why it's called New Chinatown and not Ancient China or Old China. The idea of having a Chinatown in China sounds completely bizarre anyway. Within the massive compound, there is a red-tinted room with a bar, looking somewhere between *Cabaret* and *Boogie Nights*, manned by seated and sleeveless bar

beauties. At the back there is also a bowling alley, a disco chamber, and a warmly lit and glitzy club with more than 60 comfy, spacious and affordable karaoke rooms.

Students at Melody karaoke bar, Beijing, China.

If New Chinatown is an almost affordable venue for the average Beijingers, there is also an exclusive made-in-China French château, the Zhang-Laffitte. In the early 1990s Zhang Yuchen, a former Red Guard turned real-estate developer, built the first high-class villas in the suburbs of Beijing. To promote his new thousand-villa complex, Zhang came up with the brilliant idea of copying a seventeenth-century French château, Maisons-Laffitte. With help from the Chinese architect Liu Peirong, the Zhang-Laffitte turned out to be Disneyland China at its best: a French château with Vatican colonnades and two symmetrical annexes 'borrowed' from Fontainebleau. The interior consists of golden *faux* baroque with a karaoke next to the wine cellar.

In post-reform China, Disneyfication and karaoke frenzy go hand in hand. To help make them forget the nightmare of the 'Tiananmen Incident' in 1989, billions of Chinese have since been told to get rich quickly.

The majority, however, have neither power nor the right connections: for them getting rich quickly simply means a visit to one of China's latest theme parks or a night at karaoke. The many large karaoke venues in China, some lavishly designed, tend to be dimly lit and are full of all kinds of kitsch, from fake Chinese antiques to plastic tulips or a calendar painting of the English countryside. One high-class karaoke place in Shanghai even had fake Carrara marble slabs as well as huge bas reliefs of dragons and deer, dotted with golden cornucopias. A large water feature with fat, auspicious carps swimming in it graced the entrance hall. If the future seems uncertain, in the virtual, artificial space of Disneyland or karaoke every dream comes true: an experience of a glorious past, a journey to the West or into the promised land, and a song of unfulfilled love and ambitions. As Disneyfication sweeps across the country, karaoke has become a fundamental way of life.

In the late 1980s one of the most popular songs was the patriotic 'Descendants of the Dragon', but since the 1990s everyone's dream song has been 'Evening Primrose', originally made famous by the controversial Sino-Japanese singer/actress Yamaguchi Yoshiko in the 1940s. More widely known as Li Xianglan in China, she was born in Manchuria and made her name during the war years, but afterwards she was arrested as a spy

Karaoke night, Beijing, China.

and traitor by the Chinese Nationalists and arraigned before a war crimes tribunal, although soon released. Ironically, 'Evening Primrose', a song reflecting the decadence of wartime Shanghai, has become one of the most popular songs in post-revolutionary China:

While all flowers have gone to sleep, the fragrance of evening primroses is still with me. I love this boundless and indistinct night; I love the songs of nightingales; but most of all I love the flower-like dream. Holding a bunch of primroses, I am intoxicated by it. Oh Primrose, as I sing for you, you have completely occupied my mind.

A man enjoying his karaoke time. Hong Kong, China.

Young or old, poor or rich, urban or rural, for billions of Chinese in their boundless and indistinct night, the microphone is indeed the only thing they can hold. They have found their sustenance in karaoke, even if they are not quite sure whether there will be bread or milk tomorrow. (Bread and milk were two things Lenin promised to the hungry Soviet masses in 1917, and again in 1921.)

The rise of karaoke in China coincided with the start of the economic boom of the early 1990s. It was Chen Xiuhong from Guangxi who spotted the opportunity to make a fortune from it. As one of the few who seized the prospect presented by Deng Xiaoping's economic reforms, after initial discussions with a Japanese businessman Chen determined to bring karaoke to millions of Chinese homes. China was then going through rapid social change and modernization was the height of fashion. For the average Chinese family at the time, being 'modern' meant having a colour television and Japanese home appliances or entertainment systems. Since imported goods were scarce, counterfeits were widely acceptable and readily affordable. Chen decided to market karaoke as a modern Japanese product, packaged in a piece of modern equipment with hundreds of popular Chinese and foreign songs.

His machines became an overnight hit. Suddenly a karaoke machine became the must-have item for millions of Chinese families: for those in the big cities it was almost a disgrace not to have KTV (Karaoke Television) at home, while the magic tunes produced by the giant karaoke machine sounded 'scientific' and 'modern' to villagers in the remote hinterland – and something 'scientific' could mean an escape from the village.[2] For people used to hearing Marxist jargon sung through loudspeakers, karaoke has become the new media for the new dogma. Syrupy pop songs, video footage of girls in long white dresses and young men in tuxedos running in slow motion through clouds of dry ice, or romping through the tourist sites of Taiwan, Hong Kong, or Paris – these have become the true representations of 'Socialism with a Chinese twist'. But the best thing about karaoke is that ordinary Chinese can also enjoy the privilege of holding the former symbols of power: the remote control and the microphone.

Having made his fortune from the karaoke business, Chen Xiuhong used the profits to build a property empire, and this in turn generated the cash to pay for his goose liver pâté factory. Dubbed the 'King of foie gras' in China, he is now the country's main producer of goose liver pâté. The production of his factories equals one third of all that made in France and, owing to his cheap labour costs, his pâté is now a real threat to the French varieties.[3]

Since 2004 Chen has refused to speak about his involvement in the Chinese KTV business. On 1 March 2004 the operators of some 12,000 entertainment outlets in more than fifty cities across China, mostly karaoke bars and clubs, received a letter issued by two law firms in Beijing. On behalf of more than fifty music clients in China and abroad, including EMI, Warner, Universal, Sony and Rock Records, the letter demanded that the named outlets should pay compensation for using copyright material without authorization. In line with China's laws and regulations, the letter urged the recipients to 'adopt immediate measures to stop the infringement, and compensate our clients for their economic damage' within three days of its receipt. The letter also warned of possible legal action based on the evidence acquired if nothing was done within seven days of receipt.

Some months previously, New Chinatown and Melody in Beijing and an outlet of Cashbox, a giant karaoke chain in South-east Asia, had been among the first to face legal action brought by various recording companies. The story hit the news headlines as the upcoming ruling about intellectual property rights could decide the fate of the KTV industry nationwide. In December 2003 the Beijing No. 2 Intermediate People's Court ruled that New Chinatown had infringed the plaintiff's copyright, thus setting a precedent. Warner had demanded 300,000 yuan ($36,000) for economic damages and 50,000 yuan ($6,000) for litigation expenses, but the court awarded only 38,000 yuan ($4,578) in compensation. Meanwhile Chinatown appealed to the Beijing Higher People's Court, claiming that, even if the three pieces in question were the creative works of Warner Music, their expenses had been paid when it purchased the entire music collection, including machines and equipment, some years before for about 1.2 million yuan ($140,000). A spokesman for Cashbox in Beijing warned that 'KTV and the music industry are complementary, like fish and water, counting on each other for upcoming consumers. If everything goes well this time, it's a good beginning to raise awareness for copyrights. However, if mediation efforts fail and litigation starts, it will be harmful to both.'[4] Public reaction was sympathetic towards the accused, arguing that, as a new technology, KTV should be treated differently from printed publications and patented products. Furthermore, there was no history in China of record companies charging for the use of their songs. The conclusion was that China is not like the rest of the world. China is unique.

Indeed in an economy that thrives on counterfeits the legal challenge seemed pointless. Besides, the international music industry seemed to have forgotten that before KTV there was no music industry in post-revolutionary China. In a centrally planned economy, music was owned by the state, it was a voice of the party, a tool of propaganda. From the late 1980s and early 1990s the KTV business facilitated the growth of the Chinese music industry, and hardly any pop stars in China today would have had a career were it not been for KTV or MTV.

Unlike in Europe or in many other parts of the world, pop concerts are still a rarity in China and government censorship has meant that the dissemination of pop music was extremely restricted.[5] KTV, however, allowed a privileged relationship between individuals and artists. It also provided a new mode, the karaoke machine, by which most popular songs were produced and consumed and became truly popular in China. It was through karaoke albums that many 'controversial' Chinese and Western pop stars became known in China. Even if the Chinese government does not approve of Madonna's songs, for example, an image of her can still appear on a karaoke DVD full of Communist revolutionary songs such as 'Oh Party, forever our loving mother'. While the music industry declining in many parts of the world owing to file sharing, in China it is on the rise, mainly because of the consumers of karaoke.

The music industry is not the only beneficiary. The karaoke business has been linked to the growth of many other economic activities in China, including prostitution. In a haunting piece entitled *Ladies*, first shown in 2000, the Chinese artist Cui Xiuwen placed a hidden camera in the toilet of a karaoke venue, pointing it at the basins and big mirror of the communal area, where a woman attendant dispenses towels and pieces of pink toilet paper. The women look harassed and disgruntled, rarely exchanging a word. They look at themselves in the mirror, adjust their hair and refresh their lipstick. Some plump up their breasts and tuck money away in their bras. Another Chinese artist, Wang Wending, in a recent conceptual piece called *A project comprised of one hundred projects*, writes: 'Project number 31: rebuild a flame tower on the Great Wall into a luxury Kara OK song hall. Look for some middle-aged women in the villages around the Great Wall to play-act as service girls of the song hall.'[6]

Karaoke is intertwined in the fabric of Shanghai's nightlife. It is reported that there were at least three hundred luxury karaoke establishments scattered throughout the city in the summer 2004. No ordinary Chinese person would be able to afford to spend a night in such places. Their clientele is made up of wealthy Chinese men and other East Asian males from Taiwan (one of the largest communities of foreign residents in the Chinese metropolis), Hong Kong and Korea, many of whom are permanent residents in Shanghai, or businessmen spending some time in the city. To guarantee the success of most high-level economic transactions in China, it is essential to offer a night at an expensive karaoke place to potential business partners. Such an evening can be expensive. In 2004 the rental fee for a luxury karaoke box amounted to RMB1,500 (about $175), about half the monthly salary of an ordinary clerk. On top of that, it was customary for the host to provide several bottles of whisky or other imported spirits, each costing RMB500–600 per bottle, together with expensive teas, snacks of dry meats and fruits and several boxes of imported cigarettes. At least RMB300 (about $35) is necessary to 'hire' a female hostess. These women are known in Chinese as *sanpei xiaojie*, literally 'three accompaniment miss', referring to their role as hostesses at singing, dancing and eating establishments.

In theory, there is no overt prostitution at karaoke establishments in China. The sum mentioned above only 'buys' the woman's presence in the karaoke box, where she may sing duets with her patron and engage in small talk or light 'petting'. One regular customer told us that it is up to the women whether they decide to 'go further' at the end of the evening – not necessarily for money. This may have been that person's individual experience or, more likely, a way to prettify a very different reality. In fact, despite China's ban on prostitution and occasional crackdowns in cities throughout the country, entertainment venues from karaoke bars to five-star hotels offer under-the-table services to wealthy male clients. Interestingly, some luxury karaoke and massage parlours in Shanghai stand out in the sex service industry because they target specific expatriate groups, namely men from Japan, Korea, Taiwan, Hong Kong and Singapore.

During one of our visits to a luxury karaoke venue in Shanghai, with a male friend in tow, the host invited a group of 'girls' to the room so that we could 'choose one'. Despite the strange situation – us, in the midst of a group of wealthy Hong Kong businessmen, being invited to choose a professional hostess in a luxury karaoke room – we decided to play it cool. Unlike the three women already in the box, the one we ended up choosing was fairly new to the job. She was born outside Shanghai and still retained some of her naïveté. After a short while, however, she placed her hand firmly on our friend's inner thigh, only to quietly withdraw it when, after some time, he did not show any response. Eventually someone sang a duet with her and she proved herself a good and effective singer. She told us she had come to Shanghai with her boyfriend, who had eventually left her to fend for herself. She was now hoping to meet someone else who could take care of her. Meeting a man at a karaoke box, one who might take them as *taitai* (concubines) or at least be a regular client, is what some of the women working in karaoke venues desire.[7]

In her recent book *China, Sex and Prostitution: Telling Tales*, Elaine Jeffreys recounts the life and concerns of her friend X, a rural migrant worker who had found work as a 'hostess' in what was then (1993) the flourishing market of karaoke and dancing venues in Beijing.[8] At first X liked her job for a variety of reasons. Her job as a hostess did not imply any explicitly sexual service and she was paid a 'basic salary' based on the tips her male patrons gave her; this meant that she enjoyed relative freedom in choosing her working hours and means. She was also happy to be working in the 'entertainment business' and regarded herself as lucky to be enjoying dancing and singing for free. Soon though, she was in trouble. The men were constantly looking for new faces and for girls prepared to offer 'extra services'. Eventually the Beijing Cultural Bureau banned 'hostess' activities. Initially, the police were light-handed with both karaoke owners and workers, but after a while a special task force was put together to investigate all 'hostessing' activities carried out at karaoke venues, which were regarded as a 'known front' for prostitution. That may well have been the case, if the contents of a controversial report published in the February 1994 issue of *Asia.INC* are true. The article claimed that the majority of the exclusive clubs and karaoke bars/brothels in Shanghai were owned, wholly or partly, by the Public Security Bureau (China's national police force) and by the People's Liberation Army.

Whatever the truth of the matter, on 17 September 2001 the Ministry of Public Security launched a three-month campaign to 'rectify' the entertainment industry and the police started raiding karaoke venues almost nightly. By mid-October, according to a report in the *China News Digest* (7 October 2001), the police of Guangzhou had closed more than eight thousand of the estimated twenty-thousand karaoke bars in the city. A week earlier, according to the report, the *Southern Metropolis News* had sponsored an exposé of Guangzhou karaoke venues that were disregarding the 'rectification' campaign. The police subsequently raided the establishments with the paper's reporters in tow, who wrote that, 'When bar owners

A karaoke bill-
board in China.

got wind of what we were up to they called to beg for mercy and asked us
not to expose their illegal activities but we sternly refused.' The Shanghai
municipality was among the first to issue a ban on drug abuse, gambling
and prostitution in most types of entertainment venues, including video
arcades, karaoke bars, beauty salons, teahouses, bars, hotels, saunas and
massage parlours. The ban led to several karaoke venues shutting down. A
few years later, however, the karaoke venues were back, including those
offering 'hostess' services, though with a newly added touch of discretion.
Meanwhile, some karaoke joints have decided to rename their *sanpei xiaojie* as 'Disc Jockeys' or 'Uniformed Waitresses'.

On an upper floor of a tall building in Huaihai Road, one of the
busiest, brightest and fanciest roads in Shanghai, is a luxury karaoke
establishment we visited one evening shortly after the campaign against
karaoke places had begun to quieten down. The place was huge, with
dozens of boxes and even a communal bar with a live show. Mobile phones
went off constantly as the hostesses were exchanging text messages.
Armed with a small camcorder, we tried to shoot some material discreetly,
but two very angry men soon assailed us, shouting and threatening us

Dancer at the 'Club 2R' karaoke, Guangdong, China.

until we showed them that everything we had filmed had been erased. So those blurred images vanished, but not their memories.

The exterior of another karaoke venue we visited clearly displayed all the signs of a posh establishment. There were no bright neon-lit karaoke or KTV signs in sight. The building could have been anything from a fancy restaurant to a spa. As we entered, the lady concierge nodded to our male friend, not to us, and pointed him towards the lifts. There were no common spaces and the meandering corridors led directly to the private rooms.

The karaoke boxes themselves were fairly dark, air-conditioned rooms furnished with sofas and coffee tables, a computer-like console for choosing the songs, wireless microphones and a large flat screen. The glass doors were darkened and the rooms soundproofed. All personnel who entered the rooms did so with the utmost discretion and vanished soon after with little or no interaction with the people in the room. Everything seemed geared to maintaining a sense of privacy. In one establishment we visited there was a huge L-shaped sofa facing a large karaoke screen. The equipment included a few professional wireless microphones, which were passed around among the men, who sang solo or occasionally did a duet with one of the female hostesses. An attendant dressed like an in-flight hostess regularly entered the box in order to programme the new choice of songs.

In another high rise along Huihai Road, the decadent No. 8 Club is designed to resemble a 1930s club with glittering coloured lights and stylish red lanterns. The club is all about nostalgia. Here you can sing old favourites, accompanied by a real band, or waltz on the dance floor in the middle. Forget all about the noise and pollution on the streets outside and the stress of daily life. Simply enjoy the singing and the feeling of utter decadence. Occasionally some 'lucky' rich men might even find glamorous *taitai* to take home. As a regular to the club enthused, 'This is the way to live!'

Indeed karaoke is now at the centre of millions of Chinese lives. It has even become a way of defining every aspect of daily life from one's self-image to love, misunderstanding, relaxation, work and even losing weight. This is illustrated by the following true stories (the names, however, have been changed).

After graduation May began working in a bank. She found the work repetitive, boring and suffocating. She wanted to quit but didn't have the

Karaoke night in the town of Shilong, Guangdong, China.

A 'hostess' in a karaoke bar, Guangxi, China.

Karaoke night
in the town
of Shilong,
Guangdong,
China.

courage to do so. One day a few friends invited her to a karaoke, where she
discovered her singing talent, boosted her self-image and found confidence.
Karaoke with friends has brought joy to her life. She has since decided to
pursue a new and happier life, and is now working for a newspaper, while
taking a course on fashion design. Of course she continues to sing karaoke.

Ron is a shy 21-year-old. For some time he had been secretly in love
with Ruby. To help him express his love, his friends planned a karaoke
night in a private room for the two of them. With the help of a bunch of
flowers and a big box of chocolates, Ron sang his heart out and won the
heart of his beloved.

Years ago Leo and Ray became enemies after falling in love with the
same girl. Years later they met again at a KTV party. Their shared love for
singing has helped them to forget the past and become karaoke pals.

Jan, overstressed by work and the hectic city life, had lapsed into
silence. One day a friend took him to a KTV, where he suddenly belted out

wordless tunes. After a whole hour of shouting to himself, he felt so much better. In his own words, he has since 'learnt to relax and to live'. Karaoke has now become a weekly activity for him.

After a promotion, Lam found that colleagues in his team treated him differently. Many had become jealous and resentful. Acting on a friend's recommendation, he invited the entire team to a karaoke night. Holding the microphone, Lam deliberately sang out of tune to make a fool of himself. It immediately lightened the atmosphere and everybody suddenly became relaxed and friendly. The night turned out to be a great success and karaoke became a regular night out for the team members.

In big cities such as Beijing and Shanghai, losing weight has become the latest frenzy among the young and fashionable. A recent report claimed that singing can help one to lose weight and keep slim. Overnight those in their twenties rushed to KTV. Cashbox KTV (*qiangui*), one of the biggest KTV chains throughout China and Taiwan, even has songs with a fast beat and requiring physical movement listed as especially good for losing weight. Now some karaoke venues also offer a 'slim' fire pot or 'slim' buffet dinner, supplying the energy for lunchtime or late-night singers.

Shilong. Business-men from Hong Kong and Taiwan hanging out in a karaoke night-club.

Eating at restaurants in China is essentially a communal experience and turning up without company is regarded as socially unacceptable. Increasingly, however, office workers have to lunch on their own, either because they have to take turns for lunch or because they are sick of seeing their colleagues' faces. To solve the embarrassment, many have opted for lunchtime at KTV, where it is acceptable for strangers to share a microphone or listen to strangers singing. Besides, the price is usually low, at about $5, including food, drink and unlimited songs.

Prostitutes entertaining their clients in a karaoke club in Shanghai.

Many restaurants also have karaoke rooms. Localfood.com, a tremendously popular restaurant serving cheap food in Beijing, is generally packed most evenings. The series of karaoke rooms tucked away at the back are considered true gems. Here the karaoke is actually free: customers only pay for the food they eat and the beer they drink in order to keep up their strength for karaoke. Localfood.com has a thick book of songs including relatively recent hits in English, such as The Cranberries' 'Zombie'. The food is cheap (most dishes are under 10 yuan) and tables in the rooms are big enough to seat about fifteen people comfortably. Fans describe this place as a truly 'homey' experience.

'On the Street Where You Live'

Now available in Kunming, China: street side stardom. Entrepreneurs have set up karaoke monitors on the pavements. For just a couple of RMB, you can croon your heart out, with music and visuals provided on a screen beside you. It always attracts a crowd of onlookers, so you even get an audience.

An American businessman who was passing said: 'I was drawn by this weird sound, which I assumed was a mutt-strangling operation for a famous dish, Kunming dog stew.'9

As a symbol of home comfort, family intimacy and personal wealth, and as an indicator of modernity, karaoke is an important aspect of life in China today and is featured everywhere. Huge billboards bearing KTV signs are placed on many city sky-scrapers. They are often inscribed with the signatures of well-known celebrities, rich entrepreneurs and important officials – another way they can show off in addition to holding a microphone. Even in the remotest shantytown, karaoke has become ubiquitous, with hand-painted advertisements adorning pagodas, street corners and tiled 'toilet-style' houses.

A night out at the gigantic Cashbox KTV has become an essential 'Chinese experience' for visitors from abroad. David Wu, a regular contributor to the local expats' column in Shanghai, recently took a visitor named Jim partying local-style. To Jim's surprise, they were led to an ornately decorated private room with an enormous television. Jim was utterly confused when handed a songbook from which to order the songs: 'We're just going to sing to each other? This isn't partying.' But by the end of evening he had not only enjoyed his local partying, he wanted to do karaoke again the next day.10

Jim was not the only foreigner converted to karaoke while in China. Anna, an Italian PhD student who lives in London, completely fell in love with it while doing fieldwork in a remote village in south-west China. Karaoke helped her to build up a relationship with the local people, who came to see her as a member of their village and a real 'comrade'; she even represented the village at a local karaoke competition.11

Karaoke for the Soul:
Karaoke and Religion

Karaoke and Buddhism

In 2004 the Cambodian government banned from national radio and television a popular love song written by Heng Bunleap, one of Cambodia's best-known singers, about a Buddhist monk who decides to disrobe, having fallen in love with a woman. 'Sik hos pros snear' ('Leaving the Monkhood for Love') had been on release for a month and was enjoying a roaring success when it was condemned as disrespectful towards the Buddhist monastic community. According to a statement by the Information Minister Khieu Kanharith, 'the meaning of the song harms the honour of other monks who devote themselves to being in the monkhood . . . therefore in order to promote Buddhism, which is the state religion and which all Buddhists across the country follow, the ministry would like you immediately to stop playing the song.'[1]

Before the civil war broke out in the early 1970s, Cambodia had possessed a vigorous Buddhist culture that managed to survive even the most violent attempts at annihilation, and soon reasserted itself in the years following the collapse of Pol Pot and the Khmer Rouge regime. Some Buddhist groups and associations are now playing a part in the political and economic reconstruction of Cambodian society. Thus, it is not at all surprising that the subject of the karaoke DVD, while delighting many, also offended some, who urged the government to act.

'Leaving the Monkhood for Love' is undoubtedly a sensual affair and, by Cambodian standards, leaves little to the imagination. The images

Karaoke DVD cover of 'Leaving the monkhood for love', recently banned in Cambodia.

show the bare-chested, shaven-headed protagonist frolicking with his lover in a lotus pond. Eventually the woman chooses another man, leaving the runaway monk to sing disconsolately: 'Really regret these great saffron robes. Why won't you pity me? . . . I can't think about my darling changing her mind. I promise to join the monkhood again.' This ambiguous ending is also problematic: not only is the lustful monk guilty of breaking one of the fundamental monastic rules, he even attempts to return to the monastic fold once his love story is over!

As is often the case, the ban resulted in even greater popular success for the song and the karaoke DVD among Cambodians of all age groups. Vendors at the Olympic market in Phnom Penh made fortunes selling the pirated CD version, while at the time of writing the DVD, variously described as 'one of the best DVDs I have ever seen' and 'unlike any other Cambodian DVD', was on sale for about US$12 on a website popular among Cambodian emigrants.[2]

The unholy association between karaoke and Buddhist monks, however, is not simply the product of one singer's daring imagination. According to a recent article in the *Cambodia Daily*, Um Samnang, the young abbot of the Choutika Ram pagoda in south-eastern Cambodia, was accused of singing at karaoke venues wearing civilian clothes; the monk was promptly defrocked.[3] Similar stories have emerged throughout Southeast Asia in recent years, especially in Thailand, where the popular press loves to uncover or, in some cases, invent scandals about the Buddhist clergy. Several prominent monks have been variously accused of amassing vast collections of cars, of embezzling money and property, or of slipping out at night to meet up with women in karaoke bars. Phra Pativetviset, abbot of Wat Sriboonruang in Bangkok, for example, was banished after being caught on camera, disguised in a wig, sunglasses and civilian clothes, carousing with women at a karaoke bar in his home province of Ang Thong.[4] In one of the latest developments, according to a report in *Asia Times*, one of the country's best-known monks had to flee abroad after a television show exposed his alleged relationship with a female disciple. Criticism of the clergy has become so widespread that the government has passed a 'Sangha bill' mandating between three and ten years in prison for anyone who slights or defames the Supreme Patriarch.[5]

A contributing factor in the thirst of South-east Asian audiences for stories about singing monks, whether real or alleged, is undoubtedly the perceived inseparable connections between performing karaoke, drinking and mercenary sex, forms of behaviour that are not only forbidden to monastics but are highly problematic for Buddhist practitioners in general.

In other countries the ubiquity of karaoke has elicited altogether different reactions. In the Chinese-speaking world, for example, Buddhist monks find karaoke similarly irresistible, but only as a proselytizing tool. In China, Taiwan, Hong Kong, Singapore and among Malaysian Chinese there is a growing appetite for karaoke VCDs and DVDs of both traditional Buddhist chants and of newly composed songs of Buddhist inspiration and content. These audiovisual materials vary greatly in both content and appearance. Some are explicitly aimed at Buddhist lay devotees, while others target a more generic and composite audience who either seek some spiritual solace at home or, especially in the case of South-east Asian Chinese, want to feel somehow connected with traditional Chinese culture or with their 'Chinese identity'. Many Malay Chinese listened to cassette tapes of Buddhist music in the 1970s, and more recently to DVDs, because it reminded them of their Chinese roots. The music was also considered helpful in scaring bad spirits and ghosts away from their houses.[6]

Chinese Buddhists' use of the mass media for proselytizing purposes is certainly not a new phenomenon. Throughout history Buddhists in China have been particularly effective at adapting or even devising specific technologies in order to preserve and spread Buddhist teachings, particularly in written form.

The VCD *Fanbai kala* OK *jiaochang*, or 'Buddhist Chant Kala OK singing instructions' ('OK' is a common Chinese transliteration of 'karaoke'), is an intriguing example of the production of karaoke videos

Cover of a CD of Buddhist karaoke distributed in China and Taiwan.

by Chinese Buddhist groups. The video displays traditional iconographic motifs, including images of the Buddha, lotus flowers and incense braziers. These are treated by deploying cinematic special effects such as fades, split screens and page-turners. In terms of musical content, the vocal delivery remains fairly traditional with choral singing punctuated by traditional percussion instruments (*faqi*). The 'educational' religious element is obvious in the choice of pieces that receive the 'karaoke treatment' – all the common hymns from the Chinese daily liturgy.

Fanbai kala OK *jiaochang* is produced and distributed by the Buddha's Light International Association (BLIA), a society bringing together monastic and lay members of the Taiwanese Buddhist association Foguangshan. The association logo appears constantly throughout the video. BLIA was created by the charismatic Buddhist monk Xingyun, the founder and patriarch of Foguangshan in 1991. Its main purpose is to give lay devotees the formal means to play a leading role in promoting the Buddhist dharma. BLIA has hundreds of thousands of members organized into 110 regional headquarters and chapters worldwide; its main headquarters recently moved from Taipei to Los Angeles. In many respects the international network operated by Foguangshan and BLIA far exceeds that of any other Buddhist organization in the world. The production of karaoke materials is consistent with the organization's policy towards the distribution of popular materials for proselytism. In fact, Foguangshan's literature often states that Master Xingyun has been keen on deploying audiovisual materials for educational and proselytizing purposes since the late 1950s. The master famously declared that 'Buddhism must be directed to the masses, it must be popularized and made artistic'.

Foguangshan and BLIA have a very positive attitude towards entertainment, and especially music and singing, regarding them as a possible means to attract converts to the Buddhist fold. Modern communication technologies and the mass media are considered perfectly legitimate means by which to popularize the Buddhist message. As well as publishing books and magazines, Foguangshan produces vast numbers of cassettes, videos, karaoke VCDs, CDs and CD-ROMs. It also owns satellite television channels and radio stations.[7] Although neither Foguangshan nor BLIA have an official presence in China, for political reasons, their audiovisual materials are certainly available there and can be found in a number of commercial outlets, including state-owned bookshops and audiovisual shops, as well as through retailers near or within monastic premises. It is now becoming fairly common for karaoke videos of Buddhist chanting, such as the one described above, to be played within monastic premises, especially in the shops of religious paraphernalia by the main entrance.[8]

The phenomenon of Buddhist karaoke is not confined to traditional chanting. The VCD *Baiyi Guanyin linggan zhenyan* ('White-robed Guanyin's true words of inspiration'), for example, contains new musical compositions for a rather confusing mixture of traditional and electronic instruments. The vocal parts consist of an unconventional alternation of male and female voices and the running text is written in blue (men singing), red (women singing) and green (male and female voices together), a convention taken from karaoke 'Cantopop' videos. The lyrics extol the qualities of Guanyin, one of the most popular figures of the Chinese Buddhist pantheon. Its popular success owes much to its combination of devotion to the goddess with the modern feel of a karaoke VCD. Several websites present the work of performers and composers of new Buddhist music. BuddhaNet Audio, which promotes the works of the Singaporean Daniel Yeo, offers downloadable 'Buddhist songs' in MP3 format, several of which have a karaoke version. The songs bear inspirational titles like 'Journey of Realization', 'Mundane Attachment' and 'Bond Free', while the 2003 collection borrows its title from the explicitly Buddhist recommendation to 'Come Forth'.[9]

Christian karaoke

If karaoke thrives in Buddhist lands, for better or for worse, its popularity spans other religious communities too. In 1985, in one of the first depictions of the karaoke phenomenon in the US, *Time* magazine described the presence of 'a nifty electronic device from Japan called the *karaoke*' in small churches, the University of Nebraska's Psychiatric Institute and Songmaster's Graceland Recording Studio and Singalong Shop, across the street from Elvis Presley's mansion in Memphis.[10] More recently, the American press has covered the topic extensively with articles like 'Christian karaoke music finds niche' to 'Christian karaoke sales bounce higher'. A niche market it may be, but judging by the great quantity of Christian karaoke records on sale –a simple search on the exact combination 'Christian karaoke' produced eight million Google results in June 2006 – there seems to be a huge demand for such products.

In October 2002 a business called Family Christian Stores Inc., based in Grand Rapids, Michigan, and trading through some 325 retail stores in 39 American states, released six different karaoke CDs featuring 'Christian performers'. Dozens more CDs were released in the following years. The music was intended for 'boombox karaoke', portable music players that display lyrics for singing along.[11] Frank Breeden, president of the Gospel Music Association, is not at all surprised by this success: 'It's a wonderful thing for the consumer . . . we know that people use these in settings other than just singing solos in church. Some people use them for personal enjoyment, for parties.' Even before karaoke bars became popular in the US, performers in churches were already singing to instrumental recordings of religious music (solo performance tracks or accompaniments). Thus, according to Breeden, the development was an obvious one: 'the inherent value of this product line is that it's capitalizing on something already in existence, and that is a format of music that is, by its very nature, conducive to sing along with.'[12]

Some earlier attempts at selling Christian karaoke music ran into problems finding retail outlets, but Family Christian clearly did not have that problem. According to John Van der Veen, the company's music buyer, they decided to launch this project when 'one of our vendors came to us and said: "By the way, did you know that one of the biggest retailers out there this year is going to be selling about $40 million worth of karaoke product this Christmas?", and we just kind of went, "Wow".' The first group of six CDs was targeted at girls and teenagers between the age of eight and sixteen. Each CD contains three tracks and retails for $12.98. Karaoke machines and CDs clearly have a great potential in the American 'holy leisure' market, to borrow an expression used by Troy Messenger in a different context. It is in this vein that one could read the following declaration by Family Christian's marketing director, David Austin: 'They're singing, they're having fun, but they're learning a little bit about God's word in the process and learning a little bit about some spiritual matters.'[13]

A CD cover for Gospel karaoke.

Outside North America, karaoke technology has been introduced to the theoretically more conservative setting of the Church of England. In May 2001 the *Daily Telegraph* published an article entitled 'A Nottinghamshire church has had a karaoke machine installed to improve hymn singing'. It seems that the congregation at the church of St John the Evangelist in Hucknall, Nottinghamshire, constantly failed to 'hit the right notes' after their organist moved away. They were later dealt another blow by the departure of a worshipper who brought a guitar along to accompany the singing. The vicar, the Rev. Brian Duckworth, explained their difficulties: 'Our services were getting very dull. We have a strong musical tradition here at St John's and hymns are a vital part of our worship. But I'm afraid singing unaccompanied just wasn't the same.' To solve this problem, worshippers raised £2,850 to buy a karaoke machine capable of playing about 2,400 hymns, which the vicar now expertly controls from his pulpit and can even take with him to outside services. Stephen Langford, assistant secretary of the Southwell diocese, which gave its stamp of approval to the vicar's music-making idea, has stated that the machine 'is making its mark on St John's in a way the original organ probably did 100 years ago.'[14]

The latter statement may sound a little off-hand, but the idea of singing along to Christian hymns is clearly very appealing to Anglican Christians, and not only in provincial parishes. The Anglican Church's pride in its hymn tradition, coupled with the power and user-friendliness of this technology, may lie at the heart of the seemingly bizarre combination of congregational Christian worship and karaoke machines. The scale of the phenomenon may be appreciated when reading the website devoted to the BBC's Sunday hymn-singing TV programme, 'Songs of Praise'. Running for more than forty years, the programme 'has visited all five continents of the world [and] can rightfully lay claim to being the world's largest Karaoke.' A sort of interpreter's sense of ownership of the sonic material at hand, which seems intrinsic to the idea of karaoke, is evoked by the curators of the 'Songs of Praise' project:

> These days 'Songs of Praise' is just [as] at home in the Royal Albert Hall and Football stadiums as it is in Cathedrals and Churches. The venue may change but what remains constant is the rich variety of inspirational music, music that touches both the heart and the Soul but most importantly music that you can call your own and sing-along to.[15]

The tension between disciplining karaoke and chastising its practitioners, on the one hand, and embracing it for proselytizing purposes is common to many other contexts and places. The way in which karaoke is practised in society at large is, of course, very important, even if it is not necessarily the determining factor in religious groups' appropriation or rejection of karaoke. In Catholic Italy the website http://it.groups.yahoo.com/group/midi-liturgici/ offers MIDI and karaoke versions of *canti di chiesa* or 'church songs', a genre of pop ballads commonly sung in today's churches that emerged in the 1960s and '70s in the wake of the Second Vatican Council. In Kampala, Ugandan evangelists have found in karaoke evenings a new ally in their battle to conquer souls: in 1999 the annual gospel and evangelical extravaganza undertaken jointly by the churches was moved away from its home at the Kampala Pentecostal Church and held instead at Sabrina's Pub, a karaoke nightclub. For the Islamic Party of Malaysia, on the other hand, karaoke evenings represent a serious threat. In 2000 Wan Abdul Muttalib, state councillor in charge of local government for the state of Terengganu, declared: 'We don't allow karaoke and floor shows at nightclubs' because such entertainment could 'lead to an increase in vice'.[16] The relationship between religion and karaoke, whether regarded as a tool for evangelizing or a sinful practice, remains highly contentious.

'Naked Karaoke' and the Cowboys: *North America*

In 2004 Ryan Rowe was studying for his MBA at York University's School of Business in Toronto, Ontario. He had never been very keen on karaoke, then one Friday night he was dragged to a karaoke bar in downtown Toronto by his class's social coordinator. 'I wasn't too excited,' he remembers. 'You see, I'd been looking forward to a Friday night partying with my buddy and case competition team mate Mark Van Wart. We needed to release the stress we'd accumulated after an intense week. Karaoke didn't seem to fit the bill.' When they finally arrived at the bar, he was even more disappointed:

> Where we ended up was on the second floor of a building on Bloor Street. I didn't know what to make of it. It looked like a cheesy little hotel that rents rooms by the hour to couples. There were black leather couches in the lobby and pictures of Asian celebrities and models on the wall . . . I'd never been in a place like this. I've never sung karaoke. And a karaoke bar is probably the last place I'd choose to spend my Friday night. Especially when you have to pay by the hour at $25 for a small-sized room, $45 for a medium, and $60 for a large.

They rented a small room the size of a cleaner's cupboard. As the night progressed, Ryan started to feel better:

> These little rooms are really cozy, though, and you quickly get into the mood. The room's all set up so you can create your own playlist from

hundreds and hundreds of songs and keep going for hours on end. Our group of seven was a pretty cool one too ... We ordered a few drinks and it wasn't long before we were all wailing like alley cats on a fencepost. What a fantastic way to get comfortable with new people and make new friends! Some great talent among us, too – especially Mag, who I think should audition for 'Canadian Idol'. She wasn't too flattered by that compliment, though, I wonder why? We went through a lot of old 80s songs, and classic stuff like 'Hotel California', 'Brown-eyed Girl', and 'Billy Jean'. The accompanying videos were so cheesy it was hard to keep from cracking up while singing, not to mention the fact that I couldn't keep a tune if it was worth my life. How did you guys put up with me? ... The night was a blast and I'm glad I gave it a shot.[1]

From the early 1990s karaoke fever from Asia hit Toronto. It encountered little hostility in this North American city and was embraced by many local musicians, who incorporated it into the existing local music scene. Jeff Healy, a renowned jazz musician who was presented with a lifetime achievement award by the Maple Blues Society of Canada, included karaoke as a key feature when he opened his night-club on Bathurst Street in downtown Toronto. When asked why he introduced karaoke nights to what is now considered one of the city's best music venues, he explained to Canada's *National Post*: 'A lot of very good singers who haven't landed in a band yet get discovered at karaoke ... It will give me a chance to hear a lot of talent and play with a lot of different people.' He wanted to give emerging talent 'a little push' and hoped that young musicians would hang out and get advice from seasoned veterans.[2]

Karaoke is now one of the most popular entertainments in the city and there is even a Toronto Karaoke Meetup Group with at least 70 members. This was founded in 2003 by Jonah Libster, who became a huge fan of karaoke at university and even started a karaoke bar on campus. For Jonah there is nothing more enjoyable than karaoke with 'good people and being a part of great music'. The club's mission statement says that it is not a 'Pop Idol' show, but 'created to get people together who love great music and love being a participant'. In the beginning the group met in public karaoke venues; it was fun, but the problem was that people had to wait forever to get to sing. The group decided to hire private rooms in karaoke boxes to allow more participation from its members and also give the shyer singers a bit more confidence. Since its launch the 'meetup group' has organized more than fifteen events. Its members include Pierre, who was introduced to karaoke in 2001 and now describes himself as a 'song and dance Karaoke wild man' who loves alternative 1980s and new swing; among his favourites are A-Ha, Soft Cell, Talking Heads, Depeche Mode, the Brian Setzer Orchestra, the Cherry Poppin' Daddies, Bachman-Turner Overdrive, the Doobie Brothers and Supertramp.[3]

As well as the Toronto group, Jonah has also founded karaoke 'meetup' groups in East York, a northern suburb of Toronto, and in New York City, where his family lives. There is also a Toronto Japanese Language 'meetup' group.

Japanese 'meetup' groups are another phenomenon that has been sweeping across the Pacific over the past ten years. There are at least 234 Japanese Language 'meetup' groups across the world, from Brisbane to London. As well as learning and practising the Japanese language, these groups live for their karaoke nights. In March 2005 a message was sent around to all members of a Vancouver 'meetup' group called Krazy Karaoke:

> Time to let loose the kraziness . . . lets all be kichigai and let the good times roll. We will go back to Fantacity unless an alternate suggestion is presented. Lets try dinner at the karaoke place this time, we can all chip in and order some appys or order our own individual items.

The night, according to the group report, was 100 per cent positive and fun. A mix of culture and music provided a space for Japanese and English speakers to interact and take part in an environment defined by karaoke.[4]

The principle used successfully in South-east Asia for English language teaching has quickly been adapted in the West, as the Japanese language 'meetup' groups demonstrate. Globalization is not simply

Americanization. Rather, it involves a constant movement of people, goods, culture and ideas, from East to West, from the New World to the Old. While karaoke might have originated in Japan, it has certainly become global: each country has appropriated karaoke into its own existing culture, a process illustrated by *Karaoke Cowboy*.

Karaoke Cowboy, released in January 2003, is Trevor Mills's second album, produced with his father Paul Mills, a veteran producer. A multi-talented musician, Trevor has been a part of the Toronto folk music scene since his childhood and more recently he has also been hosting New Folk nights at Hugh's Room in Toronto. According to Rachel Jagt, a music reviewer in Canada, 'Karaoke Cowboy' (the title track of the album) is a country ode to karaoke, featuring a folk gospel choir comprising Finnan, Dave Rogers, Candace Shaw, Parry and Claire Jenkins in the choruses towards the end. It has a relaxed and impromptu feel about it.[5]

Trevor is a well-known advocate of folk music:

> His friendly air and focused ethic are as inviting and refreshing as his song writing. He's a born entertainer with a knack for making people feel at ease. In concert, armed with an acoustic guitar and an expressive voice, his songs will alternately leave you laughing, crying, thinking, smiling and inevitably singing along.[6]

'Karaoke Cowboy' is a song about Trevor and his audiences. The words reveal a great passion for karaoke among the widest audience in Canada, including true devotees of country music. Trevor finds that karaoke makes people laugh, cry, think, smile and sing along and it seems to be the perfect match for his own sense of what music should be doing in today's Toronto. On the outskirts of the city, karaoke has even become a part of the Highland Creek Heritage Festival in Scarborough, which is now known as the karaoke capital of Canada.

According to Peter Styles, a well-known karaoke host, karaoke is nothing strange to Canadians. Amateur singing contests have been a regular feature of many night-clubs across Canada, from British Columbia to Quebec. In 1975 Peter began to compete in amateur singing contests held

'Karaoke Cowboy'

There's a run down bar that Sam runs down on Main St
On the corner by the record shop that closed down in the fall
There's a dusty beat up Chevy that would carry us to town
But that Chevy just don't run no more at all

Every Thursday night is karaoke
Folks come in from all around to sing their favorite song
Don't matter what your voice is like cause if you use your heart
Then the audience will always sing along

In the corner by the juke box sits a cowboy
Years of drinking whiskey show in wrinkles on his face
No one knows how old he is or where he learned his songs
But he knows the most of any in this place

He's singing Patsy Cline, Hank Snow and Elvis Presley
And a bunch more songs by people no one really truly knows
He says that it's the karaoke singing keeps him well
But there's just one thing to know before he goes

(Chorus)

Are they singing karaoke up in heaven
Does St Peter give a whiskey to the best song of the night
Do they bounce a ball across the words of the gospel
If they do then I'll be walking t'ward that light

That cowboy went and found himself a preacher
Who said that he'll find everlasting glory in the stars
To which the cowboy said, 'I don't need any of that,
Just give me whiskey poured at karaoke bars!'

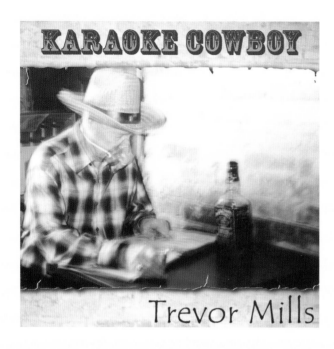

(Chorus)

He went and saw a new age hippy guru
Who could only speak of jams with Jimi, Janice, Jim and John
The cowboy said, 'well, you don't got the answers that I need
To the question that's the chorus of my song!'

(Chorus)

One day that cowboy rode towards the sunset
Gave the ferryman a dime and met St Peter at the Gate
And everywhere there's Karaoke singers singing songs
Since it's heaven well nobody has to wait

in Toronto night-clubs, either during Saturday matinee sessions or in the evenings. The contestants ranged from rank amateurs and 'wannabes' to those with real professional potential. While Peter took the competition seriously, most people only participated for fun. Peter has since turned professional, but also hosts his own amateur show. Some of the brightest names on the Canadian Country circuit, such as Debby Bayshaw, Steve Pitico and Margo Dennison, have come out of his shows. In 1985 Peter founded Stypro Records & Promotions, Canada, dedicated to the development and promotion of Canadian talent, including the personal training of prospective karaoke hosts. Peter himself continues to perform as a professional karaoke host, six nights a week, across different locations in Toronto.[7]

One of his regular dates is at the Melody Bar in the Gladstone Hotel, which has a capacity of about a hundred and which fans have voted the best karaoke venue in Toronto. One of the events the Melody offers is the Karaoke Superstar Contest, which runs for four weeks after the New Year. For the first three weeks fifteen contestants sign up on contest night to perform one song. This stage is held between 9 and 10 pm and audience response is measured by an automated 'Gladstone applause-o-meter'. The top six performers are announced at 1 am and each then performs a second song. The three singers with the highest audience response are then selected to proceed to the final; the fourth finalist (a wild card) is chosen by Peter. The event is hugely popular and every week the place is packed with the young and artsy Queen Street crowd as well as regular bar patrons.

The karaoke contest is not unique to the Melody Bar, but has become a regular feature in Toronto night-clubs. Indeed, since 2002 it has become impossible to avoid karaoke night-clubs or bars in Canada's major cities. The Bovine Sex Club on Queen Street, voted the best Hetero Bar in Toronto, has listed Kickass Karaoke night on its monthly calendar. It's a hot, hot event, so hot that people often end up wandering around wearing nothing but their cowboy hats. On those nights Bovine is completely packed, filled with yahoos fuelled to bring the house down. Favourite songs at Kickass Karaoke nights range from Meat Loaf's 'Paradise by the

Karaoke superstar contest

Scientifically Audience Judged by our patented Gladstone
applause-o-meter
You voted us 'the best' now we're looking for Toronto's karaoke
superstar . . . Step on up to the mic . . . we're looking for the
whole package!
Do it at the Gladstone with Karaoke host Peter Styles . . .
Top 4 finalists each week Jan 06, 13, 20
will proceed to final sing-off Jan 27
when they will battle it out for grand cash prize of $1000!
2nd prize $250.00 Shopping Spree at Eaton Centre
3rd prize $150.00 Shopping Spree at Eaton Centre
Contest held each week in Gladstone's Melody Bar
starting at 9:00 p.m.

Dashboard Light' to REM's 'Losing My Religion' and David Bowie's 'Space Oddity'. Participants may include multi-talented individuals capable of performing the complete round of Madonna's songs or a seemingly quiet librarian who belts out tunes by Heart, Pat Benatar and Starship. There are also punks and those into fetishes. As the night progresses, people often start to shout and substitute their own improvised lyrics. One observer summed up her reaction to karaoke at Bovine:

I couldn't help but think, 'Karaoke kills.' It kills that sulky anti-authoritarian stance and gives people a reason to yell. It's a rehabili-tative practice. It kills the will to get one's genitals pierced. Every penitentiary in Canada should have a karaoke machine, as music really does have the power to soothe the savage breast.[8]

Karaoke does not only 'kill', however, it also unites people and comforts souls. This is especially true for the East Asian and Vietnamese communities in Toronto. Asian karaoke venues have sprung up in the past few years to cater for the growing populations originally from China, Korea, Japan and South-east Asia. Many are located near the ethnic shopping malls or restaurants and provide an invaluable source of entertainment for the Asian communities. They are also major businesses among the communities in their own right.

Participants at most of these karaoke joints are expected to take their turn at performing and to enjoy each other's singing, regardless of the quality of performance. Thus karaoke enhances social bonding: community is the key. At these venues there is often a sense of group solidarity, a 'membership', that gives all participants a feeling of shared identity, security and mutual support. In this respect karaoke plays a vital role in integrating people in these communities and linking them with their cultural roots; it offers them an opportunity to meet other immigrants and sing songs in their language and from their homeland. The constantly updated VCDs give everyone an opportunity to catch up with the latest trends, fashions and other aspects of pop culture back home. Asian food and drinks are also served in these establishments, making them another venue for social gatherings, complementing ethnic malls and restaurants.

A group of American Chinese enjoy a good time at karaoke with friends. Sawtelle, California.

While some may consider karaoke an unsophisticated form of entertainment, the young and trendy in the Asian communities, however, regard karaoke as a high-tech aspect of the modern world. Like mobile phones, the bigger screens, most up-to-date mikes and latest gadgets are forms of fashion accessory and symbols of status. The particular class of karaoke bar a person frequents also becomes a marker of that person's worth.[9]

It would be a mistake to view all karaoke venues as ubiquitously cheesy and tacky or to think that there is only one kind of karaoke. Clearly in a country the size of Canada there is room for karaoke to have many different faces. The Royal Vancouver Porn Society in British Columbia has recently embarked in a series of 'Pornaoke' evenings. The secretary of the association, the filmmaker Sean Q. Lang, explains:

The whole reason for having a formal porn club was simply the ludicrousness of taking pornography and having an interest group . . . You think of interest groups as organised committees with political objectives. So what more of a ridiculous organisation could there be than a society dedicated to watching porn? . . . [Pornaoke is] a cross between karaoke and old porno movies. The film is shown silently and people volunteer to improvise the sounds and words of the red-hot performances. In true porno style, the scenes range from awkward living-room drama to full-throttle action – often in a matter of mere seconds. When we take it out to a bar or a club, we'll have a DJ spinning music for each scene. We're gonna go international with this. I think the interest is there.[10]

As predicted by the Royal Vancouver Porn Society, pornaoke has crossed the Atlantic and found a new home in Scottish night-clubs. In December 2004 a club in Edinburgh introduced pornaoke to Britain. Participants are asked to provide the soundtrack for silent porn films, supplying grunts, screams and groans. Prizes are awarded for the best solo performance and group sex categories. 'To be honest I was not quite sure what to make of it at first', the Pornaoke Lounge's compère, the stand-up comedian Garth Cruickshanks, explained, 'but the people taking part really enjoyed themselves and understand that it is just harmless fun.' The evening was a success, even if the group Scottish Women Against Pornography remained unconvinced of its harmlessness.[11]

Canada has yet more varieties of karaoke to offer further east. A reporter for the *Montreal Mirror* named 'Scott C' makes the point that Karaoke Culture 'in all its forms is alive and well in Montreal'.[12] For anyone in Montreal wanting to be a star for a night there is always Cheers at 1260 McKay, where every Tuesday night the karaoke is hosted by Dan Schwinteck. Being able to sing is here really essential; those who don't make the standard, though, can watch the game on TV screens or climb upstairs to the pool game. Karaoke may not be the only attraction, but it's a barrel of fun just the same and perfect for the tipsy songbird. At 115 Ste-Catherine E, in the Village, Cabaret Mado's Sunday-night Star Search with

MC Miklos is a serious business. Performers must sign up in advance for one of three categories – drag queen, chanteur/chanteuse or variety – and compete for prizes, advancing from week to week until one lucky crooner has a chance to win a trip to Spain. Then there is Kagopa at 6400-B St-Jacques W, which is open twelve hours a day, seven days a week, and is dedicated to karaoke and nothing else. Private rooms may be rented by the hour, each equipped with an L-shaped couch, karaoke machine, sound system and multiple microphones. Authentic Korean cuisine and alcohol are available and, combined with total privacy, may be all you need to find your private voice.

For those who prefer intimacy there is Le Tycoon Karaoke, situated at 96 Rue Sherbrooke W, a cosy little place Cocos bought in 1990 during karaoke's heyday in Montreal. Cocos insists that he has never sung in his bar, claiming to be afraid of his own voice. While most modern karaoke technology employs CDG (compact disc graphics), CDV (compact disc video) or DVDs, Cocos prefers the original Laserdisc format. Le Tycoon is comfy, intimate and not at all intimidating, and it has a sound system to die for.

Unlike Cocos, Dan Schwinteck loves to sing. He is a popular Montreal karaoke host and the owner of Schwin-Tech Karaoke, which supplies hosts, DJs and rentals throughout the region for karaoke joints, weddings, bar mitzvahs and corporate functions, as well installing and maintaining systems. Dan's conversion to karaoke followed the rousing audience reaction, admittedly helped by drink, to his rendition of 'Pretty Woman' in a karaoke bar while on holiday in Florida in 1989. He just knew he had to bring the feeling back to Montreal.[13]

Dan is not the only one to have experienced something like a divine revelation. John Dunn, the 'Karaoke Guy' in Wasaga Beach, Central Ontario, also saw the light in a Florida bar while on holiday and was hooked at once. After returning to Hamilton he decided to start his own karaoke place and spread the 'gospel'. In time he left Hamilton with a mini van loaded with karaoke equipment and opened the Nitestar Karaoke at Wasaga Beach: 'After one weekend of karaoke people were hooked! The town loved laser karaoke right away . . . I have been at the Beach for the last

10 unforgettable years and have one of the largest song libraries in Canada.'[14] John eats and sleeps karaoke, claiming to love it 'with all my heart'.

Florida, the paradise of the American Dream, has also acted as the road to Damascus of karaoke for many Americans. There are at least fifty karaoke venues in central Florida alone where ambitious American amateurs can exhibit their singing skills. The karaoke craze has also spread across the south of the state at hurricane speed with no sign of abating. Seven days a week, 365 days a year, karaoke blows from bar to bar, restaurant to restaurant. At Singers Karaoke Klub in Pompano Beach, dubbed the 'Biggest Little Karaoke Bar in South Florida' by its management, sleepless karaokers can walk in at 4 am to indulge their inexplicable hankering to belt out Beyoncé's 'Naughty Girl'. Singers provides customers with real American service offered with a big smile. 'Choice' is believed to be the essence of America, and Florida is certainly the land of choice for karaoke: at Singers customers can 'shake it like a Polaroid picture' with their 'friends in low places', taking their pick from Sinatra and The Doors to Britney, Shaggy and Rob Zombie.[15]

If Singers boasts being the 'biggest', Maria's at Bonita Springs claims to be the best in the area. Owned by Mary and David Lessnau, Maria's has invested $21,000 in karaoke equipment and CDs. Besides a computerized system and Bose speakers, Maria's has over 860 karaoke CDs and songbooks with over 11,000 titles catering for every music taste. The Lessnaus make sure their songbooks are constantly up-to-date, so that customers will always find the latest hit songs as well as the older favourites. Mary has a country singing background and acts as hostess, while Dave takes care of technical details to make customers sound great. With Mary's skills as a hostess and the incredible sound system, the place guarantees every customer a highly enjoyable evening. Since a huge number of customers are Hispanic, Maria's offers a large selection of Spanish songs. Aspiring stars at Maria's can even record their performances on CD for only $2 per song.[16]

As well as 'choice', the land of the American Dream is also thought to provide opportunities to all. In 1996, for example, there were reports that a growing number of nudists in the Tampa area of Florida had become regulars at local karaoke venues, jumping on stage to belt out tunes in the nude. They claimed that karaoke is a perfect choice of nudists, since those used to exposing themselves in public have no problem feeling comfortable on stage. While nudists enjoyed the freedom of singing without the confines of clothes, many non-nudists loved to watch them on stage and often expressed admiration for the singers' nerve, if not for their ability.[17]

Karaoke can also be about more than just enjoyment and performance. CowboyKaraoke.com was conceived by Wayne and Cathy Desmond with the intention of bringing to Tampa Bay 'the highest calibre, classy, fair, clean, well run karaoke entertainment ever seen in this area . . . Our aim is to be the show that all others are measured against.' As one of the venues most frequently visited by the local population, Cowboy Karaoke.com also offers the services of its karaoke show and website to help the local work of the National Center for Missing and Exploited Children.

Karaoke is big business in Florida, so it is not surprising that the Japanese Itochu Corporation has chosen Florida to test its new karaoke channel cable television system. This enables viewers to select songs from a menu on their television screens. Once this has been done the music and lyrics are transmitted to their television and the sing-along can begin. The Japanese company believes that if the product becomes popular in Florida, it would soon spread nationwide.

Itochu Corp is certainly not alone in trying to cash in on Florida's Karaoke craze. The infamous Porn Star Karaoke from California also struck the Florida coast in May 2005. Also known as PSK in Los Angeles, Porn Star Karaoke began in 2003 as an event at Sardo's Bar in Burbank hosted by Wankus from KSEXradio.com. Since its inception it has become popular with all types of audience and has been featured on Comedy Central, Playboy TV and regularly on adult news and entertainment sites. According to Wankus, 'It really is a fun and safe event that mixes adult stars with fans and everyone has a blast', while a regular fan of the club has described PSK as an 'awesome' event where 'everyone is really nice, the fans are very polite and respectful and everyone is just out to have a good time.'

Fans attending the event are encouraged to bring girls with them, so the female to male ratio evens out nicely. Since PSK attracts many people from the adult entertainment industry, this also makes it an incredibly good event for performers, producers, directors, KSEX radio hosts, publicists, press people, webmasters, photographers and anyone else in the business who wants to network. As well as porn celebrities, the PSK Club has also been graced by mainstream celebrities including Drew Carey and Tommy Lee, while members of Cypress Hill have come to PSK to sing their own songs!

PSK is not the only place where karaoke has been used for social networking. When Tom Cruise went to Japan to promote *The Last Samurai*, for example, in true celebrity ambassadorial style, he took the opportunity to croon a few tunes in karaoke style with Prime Minister Junichiro Koizumi. In addition to the usual Elvis songs, the pair even performed a duo of 'I Want You, I Need You, I Love You'. Wags suggested that Cruise and Koizumi might 'get together with North Korea's Elvis look-alike dictator, Kim Jong Il, for one rousing rendition of "Give Peace a Chance"',[18] though it's perhaps more likely that Kim Jong Il would have it 'My Way'.

Besides being a tool in forging diplomatic ties, Stanton Royce in Albuquerque, New Mexico, ardently believes that karaoke can be used to strengthen employee relationships, develop team skills and promote diversity. Stanton, an MBA, was once lead singer in a rock 'n' roll band. To combine his singing talent with his professional interests, Stanton developed a form of karaoke contest for conferences and the workplace. Participants, who may come from company divisions scattered across the country or even the globe, are divided into teams containing a mix of newer staff and more senior members. Most of them may never have worked together or even know each other. In order to make a high score, team members must work together, identifying talents within the group and assigning the best person to the tasks, which include singing, dancing, making props and possibly costumes, and organizing. According to Stanton this is a low-risk method of helping company staff function better as teams of diverse individuals. Managers can observe how individuals function when required to place the welfare of the group ahead of personal interests to achieve a desired outcome.[19]

As well as building team spirit for the new global economy, karaoke is also reported to have helped create a community. *The Karaoke Show: Willy's Comedy of Errors*, which played in New York at Club El Flamingo in 2002, transferred the setting of Shakespeare's original play from Syracuse to a Chelsea night-club in New York City, while retaining the errant twins, mistaken identity and a surprising family reunion. According to Diane Paulus, the show's director, karaoke as a 'major cultural phenomenon . . . is about making a community out of the audience'. 'Creating a community in this space' was to become Diane's mission statement. She claimed that *Karaoke Show* differs from dressed-up versions of karaoke in a traditional musical theatre setting,

> because it's *actual* karaoke . . . We're not in a theatre, we're in an actual disco. We use the karaoke as part of the story – the music is seen differently because it's now part of the lens of the story, of the characters' lives, so the karaoke experience becomes changed. The theatre experience, too, is completely changed.[20]

The show had an ethnically diverse cast and drew on cultural experiences from Kung fu to hip-hop and Elvis, pulling the audience into the action to create a simulated party for everyone.

If a karaoke show is a party for everyone, then what Kamikaze karaoke has to offer is fun and an experience described by one Baltimore club as 'Bad Music for Bad People. Costumes encouraged, no skills required'. In a typical karaoke night, at a typical karaoke venue, customers are encouraged to sing whatever song they may choose. In case they turn out to be boring for some, here is the solution. Instead of letting singers choose the songs they sing the best, everyone willing to participate in Kamikaze karaoke has to sing whatever the KJ might choose for them. A large sombrero is filled with tickets, each with a ridiculous old song like 'Mony Mony', 'My Ding-a-Ling' or 'I'm too Sexy' written on the back. Singers pick up a slip and sing. Bartenders are encouraged to develop the Kamikaze karaoke concept into an event replete with strange and wild tasks, penalties and even valuable prizes. It's good for business and clients seem to enjoy it immensely.[21]

From PSK to Stanton Royce's corporate karaoke contests, *The Karaoke Show* and the Kamikaze freak show, karaoke in America is without doubt a public affair, whereas in Japan most karaoke singers practise in private boxes or with a small group of friends. Karaoke provides a dream opportunity for Americans to display their great ambition and talent in front of their fellows. Kathi Kamen Goldmark, a San Francisco book publicist who gained her early performing experience doing karaoke before helping to form the Rock Bottom Remainders, a band whose members included Stephen King, Matt Groening and Amy Tan, described karaoke's appeal in the early 1990s: 'when you do it and get into the swing of it, it's really fun. It's a way of acting out a little fantasy of being a singer.'[22] The yearning for stardom is the key to the success of karaoke in America. After all, the American dream is built on the belief that everyone can make it! Karaoke teaches people the songs they cannot sing. It helps Americans to realize their otherwise unfulfilled ambitions, even if it's only for three minutes. No wonder Americans spend over $300 million on karaoke every year.

Karaoke hit the United States in the early 1980s. At first it was popular among East Asians, nostalgic for the sounds of their homeland. They gathered at bars in Japantown, where they could sing not only Japanese songs but also Chinese, Korean and Vietnamese. But this is no longer the case, now that literally thousands of bars and clubs feature the devices nationwide. While Florida took an early lead, half of the 41 nightspots in Chattanooga, a small city in the southern state of Tennessee, now offer karaoke. In Buffalo, New York, near the Canadian border, there are at least thirty weekly karaoke bars. About a hundred amateur singers showed up at the Brass Monkey, Los Angeles's most popular karaoke hangout, to celebrate Halloween. Unlike most Asian countries, where karaoke is a strong tie that binds the family together, in America karaoke mostly plays a role similar to that of a house party, another way to socialize with friends and neighbours.

A star is born at karaoke, USA.

A karaoke contest at ABS Studio, New York, 2002.

Karaoke is America's fastest growing entertainment medium and has its own national magazine. *Karaoke Singer* is produced by LA Communications in Rochester, New York, and is a sister publication to *Mobile Beat*, the magazine of the mobile DJ industry. The magazine is packed with tips of the trade, new products to enhance readers' enjoyment of karaoke, and the latest song releases from all the major karaoke software manufacturers. Feature articles, mostly written by industry professionals, cover everything from voice lessons to how to launch a recording career.

Once regarded as tacky in 'cool' California, karaoke is now the trendiest thing to do. It has become a symbol of modernity, a modern vice to help keep alive some dying traditions and cultures. Daniel Azjen and his son Roman are two enthusiasts who are using karaoke as a way of preserving and disseminating old Yiddish melodies. Yiddish was the language of the Jews of Central Europe, vast numbers of whom perished in the Holocaust. The Azjens have named their project Save the Music. Its catalogue, which boasts more than 7,000 songs in Yiddish and Ladino, the latter being the language of the Spanish-Jewish Diaspora, is claimed to be the world's leading collection of Yiddish records. To help a new generation learn to appreciate Yiddish music, Daniel and Roman have established a project to make the collection available via an online radio station, library and an Internet karaoke machine. According to Daniel, 'Music is the best method to bring people into the soul of something. In three minutes you have a teaching, a piece of history, something that moves your soul. You don't have to know anything.'

Dante finds karaoke a real therapy – it makes him feel better each time.

Karaoke, aka Burning Man Lite, USA.

The idea for Save the Music came to them in 1998, when Roman was working on a family history project for a high school English class. Many of the Yiddish records and books the family owned were in a poor condition and Roman realized that this something happening to all Yiddish material. The project was made possible with the help of the Web company that Daniel ran in San Diego and a neighbour's small recording studio. Roman began to clean and digitize the stacks of music sent to them by donors in Argentina, Australia, Mexico, California and New York. A karaoke version of 'Zog Nit Keyn Mol' ('Never Say'), the anthem of Jewish partisans who fought against the Nazis, is available through the project's website (www.savethemusic.com) with translations and transliterations in English, Yiddish, Spanish and French. Not content with one version, they intend to provide multiple versions of the same song, perhaps up to eight or ten renditions, by performers ranging from Chava Alberstein and Theodore Bikel to Paul Robeson and Jan Peerce, with original lyrics, sheet music and transliterations, so that new performers can learn the melodies and pass them on. Daniel feels that karaoke is an ideal medium to achieve their ends: 'We're looking to bring back the enjoyment of being Jewish that music used to generate in people – not just a tradition, not just a religion, but a happiness. If you lose the music, then you lose the spirit.'[23]

The idea of using karaoke to preserve the Yiddish cultural tradition and bring people happiness was certainly not invented by the Azjens, since in 1996 Sherri Bloomfield, from Venice, California, produced a ten-minute karaoke video of Yiddish classics accompanied by romantic archival footage of Jewish celebrations. The video consequently won the 1997 Jewish video competition and has been shown in Paris.

If, as Daniel Azjen suggests, karaoke can bring back the enjoyment of being Jewish, and ultimately happiness, then karaoke may be seen as the 'techno Zion' for Jews outside Israel. Some of those who live within Israel, however, have found their happiness in Israeli karaoke (or Hebrew karaoke), which was born in 1996 when sing-along flourished in Israel. It quickly spread to North America, as young North American Jews attempted to find their 'lost roots' and their Jewish identity. NonStop Production, a company now based in Culver City, California, produces VCDs and DVDS combining Israeli songs and video clips set against such backgrounds as the most breathtaking scenery in Israel, the Israeli defence force in action, and funny videos such as sport bloopers.

If the Japanese, Chinese and the Jews all have their own karaoke, then patriotic Americans must have theirs, too. To no one's surprise karaoke has become a vehicle for American patriotism. There is now a Patriotic Karaoke series of CDs produced by Sound Choice, a registered karaoke company in Charlotte, North Carolina. This includes country songs such as 'Where the Stars and Stripes and the Eagle Fly' and patriotic anthems like 'America the Beautiful'. Such songs are the stuff of school assemblies and baseball games, the sort of collective singing, often with the words projected for everyone to sing, that most Americans have experienced.

Just as most sports build to international tournaments, so karaoke has its annual Karaoke World Championship held in Finland. Cindy Shields, who lives in Middletown, Delaware, announced her intention of taking on the world there in 2003, even though it would mean driving nine hours to Arden, North Carolina, for the nearest regional heat to find the official US representative. Her brother, who is a KJ (karaoke DJ), first introduced Cindy to singing and that night changed her life. Since then she has set her sights on showing Europe what real American karaoke is all about.[24]

A Karaoke People: *Britain*

Although Japan and other karaoke-crazy Asian countries refused to take part in the inaugural Karaoke World Championship in Heinola, Finland, in 2003, claiming that karaoke was not like an Olympic sport, many in the West took it very seriously. While Cindy from America wanted to show off her love for her country, the first two champions were British, and both were certainly very proud of being crowned the first among a pack of 70 contestants: Danni Gadby, a 23-year-old restaurant worker, and Uche Eke, a 31-year-old stock analyst, won the women's and men's titles, respectively.

According to Malcolm McLaren, the pop impresario, self-publicist and former manager of the Sex Pistols, Britain is a karaoke nation: being British is about doing everything 'you are not' – singing karaoke in bars, eating Chinese or Japanese food, drinking French wine, dancing to Italian music, wearing Prada and Nike, listening to Cher, using an Apple Mac, holidaying in Florida and Ibiza and buying a house in Spain.[1] In 1999 he produced an autobiographical art installation entitled *The Casino of Authenticity and Karaoke*, which was exhibited in Maastricht, Paris and Karlsruhe. It carried the message of karaoke as a lifestyle. The installation consists of an interactive area, in which the visitor meets persons, events and elements from McLaren's life. Each of the four fruit machines displayed in the exhibit represents a phase in his life: the machine labelled 'Erruer Fatale' is McLaren growing up, 'DIY' is McLaren as a performer, the 'Sex Pistols' machine is his management career, and the 'Boy in the Blue Lamé Suit' represents Vivienne Westwood's shop. The cylinders of the fruit machines are linked to computers that control the projection of soundbites, video, text and music on to two walls of the room. By playing the machines, viewers can, in effect, 'play' or even 'relive' McLaren's life, as if it were karaoke. 'We live today in a Karaoke world', says McLaren, 'Tony Blair is the first Karaoke Prime Minister. He has branded the whole country.'[2]

While many might find McLaren's claim hard to swallow, only thinking of karaoke as the world of drunken, maudlin women in pubs belting out 'I Will Survive', someone who ardently agrees with McLaren is Steve Lamacq, the presenter of the influential indie radio show 'Lamacq Live' on the digital station 6Live. Inspired by McLaren's 'Karaoke Britain' and the Punk Metal Karaoke nights at Arlene's Grocery, a club in New York, Lamacq came up with the idea of a UK Punk Rock Karaoke club night. This is held in London twice a month at Upstairs at The Garage, where you can select your favourite punk classics and be backed by a proper band.[3]

Steve believes that the live band enables people to get up and relieve all the frustrations they have suffered for many years by never having been in a rock and roll band. It is much like the American adult 'Rock and Roll' camps, where for a week you can live out your fantasy of being a rock star. Whether one usually sings into a hairbrush or only joins in with less adventurous sing-alongs, the point of Punk Rock Karaoke is that people can get up on stage with a live backing band and have a really good night. At the time of writing, Londoners were still turning up regularly after some two-and-a-half years.

Lamacq's enthusiasm for karaoke is shared by many in Britain, including members of the royal family. While still at Eton, the seventeen-year-old Prince William gave a Royal Command Performance of 'YMCA' during a karaoke competition. William and forty of his classmates were staying at the Crossways Hotel in Thornley, Co. Durham, during a four-day geography field trip. Thursday was the hotel's weekly karaoke night and William suggested to the hotel owner that there should be a North vs South karaoke competition: the regulars against the Eton pupils. According to the owner, the boys thoroughly enjoyed the singing and took the competition very seriously.[4] More recently, William's younger brother Harry has been spotted giving fair renditions of the *Grease* hit

'Summer Nights' and Dexy's Midnight Runners' 'Come on Eileen' at hotel karaoke sessions.

From the royals and the Etonians down to the commoners, karaoke transcends the barriers of age, class, sex and ethnicity, and unites the British. Thousands of Brits are as passionate about karaoke as they are about football, and inventive karaoke producers have now come up with an ingenious product that combines the two passions, making it possible for fans to croon football songs in front of a giant video screen featuring highlights from matches across the decades.

Karaoke and football nights are among the most prominent features of British pub culture. According to a recent report by the Policy Research Institute in Britain, 24 per cent of men regularly watch sports on TV in the pub, 31 per cent of adults enjoy pub quizzes, and 19 per cent favour pub karaoke sessions.[5] Singing is certainly not a rare activity for British pub-goers, since the pub has historically been a popular venue for live song with people being encouraged to get up and sing, notably during the mid-nineteenth century. There were also the music halls, where the 'pop idols' of the Victorian era led choruses from the stage. Working men's clubs provided opportunities for singing somewhere between those offered by the pub and the music hall.[6] When the karaoke boom hit Britain in the late 1980s, it took little time to become established in pubs, bars and clubs, as well as at private parties and in homes around the country.

As anthropologists and ethnomusicologists still debate about the historical continuity between the British working-class singing tradition and the current karaoke bubble, the reality is that karaoke culture is a microcosm of contemporary society in general. It is no coincidence that Dennis Potter chose the metaphor as the title of one of his final plays: 'I called it Karaoke because – oh, you know the song or the story of our lives is sort of already made up for us.'[7] In an interview on Channel 4, he explained:

There is music, and you have your little line, you can sing it, and every thing is written for you and that is the way life feels to a lot of people. For some you haven't got much space, and even the space you've got, although you use your own voice, the words are written for you.[8]

Potter's 'Karaoke people' represent the mass of Britons, who see David Beckham as their idol and follow Blair as their political leader. Karaoke is a modern British way of life, nicely packaged and readily consumed, like the readymade foods from Marks & Spencer, another hit with the British dating back to the late 1980s.

When Ivor Arbiter, the leading British retailer of drums and guitars, decided to bring karaoke to the consumers, it was not from any passion for singing. Arbiter was a shrewd entrepreneur. He saw that Britain, along with the rest of the world, was moving towards a 'karaoke age' in which technology runs people's daily lives. You no longer need to think – just follow instructions, because everything is written down in a manual. Forget about hard work – simply press the remote control, or flick the switch, for every dream to come true. Technology is magic and karaoke works miracles. Whether 'do-it-yourself' or 'do it with a microphone', it creates the illusion that you have achieved something you can feel good about.

Arbiter also knew the importance of branding. In the contemporary consumer society, a brand name is a means to success. In Britain Arbiter is 'a famous name moving with the time' and recognized by cognoscenti of the music world. Even though Arbiter's karaoke machines cost two or three times more than comparable products from Asia, they have easily outsold their rivals at Dixons stores in London's West End.[9] The more one spends, the happier one is. This is a belief shared by the average brand-conscious British consumer. Even if the happiness one finds through karaoke is virtual, an Arbiter karaoke machine is tangible.

The legendary Ivor Arbiter died in 2005, but karaoke is here to stay. With the 'Pop Idol' frenzy in 2002, it suddenly seemed that everyone wanted to sing, and Woolworths ran out of karaoke machines in the weeks leading up to Christmas. One of BBC3's attractions on Christmas Day 2004 was an hour-long 'Christmas Karaoke' show, featuring a mix of pop videos and footage from the 'Top of the Pops' archives and other BBC shows. Each track comes complete with lyrics on screen so that viewers can sing along with their favourite artists. The featured songs range from Christmas classics, including the original Band Aid, the Pogues'

'Fairytale of New York' and Slade's 'Merry Christmas Everybody', through to recent hits by the likes of The Darkness and Robbie Williams.

The British love Robbie Williams. They also love copycat shows and in 2002 ITV ran a documentary series called *Copycat Kids*, a summer show at Blackpool, following the progress of its young cast, all under fifteen, from first auditions to final performances. One of its stars was Trevor Hodgson, a blonde fifteen-year-old from Kirkholt, Rochdale, whose singing voice was described as 'sweeter than chocolate'. He went on to win the £5,000 first prize in the *Manchester Evening Standard*'s Search for a Star competition in 2003 and two years later was back on ITV as a contestant in 'x Factor'.

There is money in karaoke: sometimes for gifted performers, like Trevor, but more so for promoters. Martha Lane Fox first appeared on the scene in 1998 when, at the peak of the dot.com bubble, she co-founded

BBC3's 'Christmas Karaoke' playlist, 2004

Wham: 'Last Christmas'
Mel & Kim: 'Rocking Around the Christmas Tree'
Kylie Minogue: 'Santa Baby'
The Darkness: 'Christmas Time (Don't Let the Bells End)'
Mariah Carey: 'All I Want for Christmas Is You'
East 17: 'Stay Another Day'
Jocelyn Brown & the TOTP Allstars: 'Happy Xmas (War Is Over)'
Robbie Williams & Nicole Kidman: 'Something Stupid'
Flying Pickets: 'Only You'
Tom Jones: 'Sex Bomb'
Pulp: 'Common People'
Oasis: 'Don't Look Back in Anger'
Chumbawamba: 'Tubthumping'
Right Said Fred: 'I'm Too Sexy'
Robbie Williams: 'Angels'
Frankie Goes to Hollywood: 'Relax'
The Pogues: 'Fairytale of New York'
Wizzard: 'I Wish it Could Be Christmas Everyday'
Slade: 'Merry Xmas Everybody'
Band Aid: 'Do They Know it's Christmas?' (original video)

Lastminute.com with Brent Hoberman. This online leisure, travel and gift business turned out to be a big success story and Martha became one of the hottest businesswomen in Britain. While on holiday in Morocco in May 2004, Martha nearly died in a car crash, suffering massive internal bleeding and shattering bones in her right arm, leg and pelvis. While still recovering, and after more than a dozen operations, Martha announced an ambitious project to invest in London's latest cool venue, Lucky Voice, a karaoke bar in Soho with luxury private boxes. A veteran karaoke fan ('When you have a bit of a singsong, you feel naturally uplifted'),[10] her intention was to test the market and see whether Lucky Voice, which opened in June 2005, might lead

Digital song book,
Lucky Voice
Karaoke, London.

to an explosion of karaoke bars across the city. Martha was right: Lucky Voice has transformed karaoke in the UK and made it 'cool'.

Lucky Voice occupies a basement in Poland Street and consists of nine beautifully designed, air-conditioned private rooms and a welcoming bar. The rooms are of varying size, accommodating between four and ten people. All are equipped with state-of-the-art touch screen technology for browsing and choosing from the extensive song library.

Mike and menu,
Lucky Voice
Karaoke, London.

Guests can also use the control panel to vary the lighting, including UV light, add vocal effects or summon a member of staff. There are wireless microphones in each room for those singing and percussion for everyone else. There is also a comprehensive drinks menu with an exotic 'oriental' twist and a selection of nibbles to be shared.

If Arbiter is about brand, Lucky Voice is about being 'cool'. In twenty-first century Britain, being 'cool' defines being British, and karaoke is the coolest thing in town. No celebrity party in the capital is complete without stars crooning. If it seemed everyone in Britain suddenly wanted to sing after the 2002 'Pop Idol' frenzy, in 2005 everybody wanted to be seen at a karaoke bar. Suddenly it is as difficult to get into Soho's original Tokyo-style bar, the Karaoke Box, as it is to get a table at The Ivy. Even on the night of 2 July 2005, while Live 8 was packing out Hyde Park, there was a 1980s-style karaoke party in Soho, with the admission fee donated to charity.

Karaoke has, in fact, been a huge success at charity fundraising events across the country. One example, drawing more than two thousand entrants, was Karaoke Krazy, a nationwide 'Pub Idol' show hosted in 2003 by The Hungry Horse pub chain in conjunction with Cancer BACUP, Britain's leading cancer information charity; the organizers described this as 'an ideal partnership as we both have strong orientation towards community'.

Not only charities have benefited from the karaoke craze. It has also been a blessing for taxi passengers. In Bolton, Lancashire, Kevan Jackson fitted a karaoke machine in the back of his cab in 2001, initially as a joke, but discovered his customers could not get enough of it. One passenger, Janette Ainsworth, told the *Manchester Evening News*: 'It's certainly the best cab I've been in. It's a great way to get in the mood for a night out or finish off the night on the way home.'[11]

At charity fundraising events, in taxis, churches (see chapter Five) and in all manner of circumstances, karaoke is certainly making

Karaoke duet at Karaoke Box, with Japanese onscreen lyrics, Soho, London.

its mark on the lives of millions across Britain. The contemporary nation is loaded with Dennis Potter's 'Karaoke masses', imbued with a form of nostalgia or secretly nursing a mixture of longing and aspiration that can only manifest itself through a virtual world. By consuming karaoke they find deliverance, a way to 'let it go' or 'let their hair down'. Karaoke enables them to pretend, and pretend to pretend. Potter compared the tuppenny jukebox to a therapeutic balm that cures and soothes. Even if it doesn't, it gives one the illusion of relief.

'Karaoke Forever':
Europe

Every country in Europe, communalities aside, has had its own trajectory in the process of the appropriation and popularization of karaoke technology and practices. Various factors have been responsible for these differences, including local legislation on authors' copyright, the availability of materials in the local languages, and the influence of a country's existing culture of public singing and leisure pursuits.[1]

If the Welsh appear not to need alcoholic stimulants to burst into song, the spread of karaoke in France, except in Paris, has been drenched in cognac. In 1992 John, an entrepreneurial Briton, together with a few friends, drove a small van carrying a karaoke machine to France. Every night they would throw a karaoke party in bars, discos or halls, all the way from Toulouse to the Loire valley. John's shows were part of a series of promotional tours for the Hennessy cognac brand, whose marketing executives might have taken their inspiration from Japanese businessmen, many of whom show a similar passion for karaoke and Hennessy. A typical tour would visit four or five localities in succession. Each night they would drive to their destination, set up the sound system, do the sound check and then meet up with the Hennessy representative, who would introduce the crew to the locals. 'We would go out for dinner', says John, 'and then turn up, slightly drunk, turn the thing on and jump up and go: "*bon soir!*"' At the start of the evening the crew gave a demonstration of what to do. By contract, the *animateur* had to sing a song in English and one in French to get things going. He already had a fair number of songs at his disposal, with many French songs, including classic Edith Piaf numbers, and pop tunes in English ranging from Supertramp to Sting. The quality of the videos, on the other hand, was appalling: badly shot, mostly literal illustrations of the topic at hand, such as a yellow submarine for 'Yellow Submarine'. Much material came from Japan, sometimes complete with misspellings or even phonetic spellings of words instead of the real thing.

The French audiences John encountered simply loved karaoke. They were extremely open to bad singing and, as onlookers, were far less cynical than the Parisians. After a while John became expert at making a sort of sociological assessment of a local community and its karaoke-singing potential: 'The best thing was to get into a place, have a look around and guess by the hair styles, the mustachios, the rugby shirts, what these people liked to sing, what they wanted to hear.' Sometimes John's karaoke evening was the biggest event the sleepy rural village had ever witnessed:

> They always rose to the challenge. Sometimes it was absolutely packed; it was like a concert . . . unbelievable. We used to get people dancing on the tables, everybody up and dancing, much more like a party, not the Japanese way, very formal. Sometimes it got so rowdy . . . in some places we were not allowed back.

Before John started to drive his van across the French countryside, karaoke was almost unknown in France, except for a small pocket in the south of France. Taking little credit himself, the British pioneer takes a straightforward and simple view of the immediate success of karaoke in France: 'there is little bit of exhibitionism in all of us and karaoke brings that out'.[2]

Some fifteen years after its merry beginnings, the French passion for karaoke, especially at grass-roots level, shows no signs of fading away. Writing as an anthropologist and a karaoke enthusiast, Alain Anciaux has humorously chronicled the wide popularity and development of karaoke culture in France and Belgium. Almost every karaoke bar or nightclub has its own ambience, its own karaoke philosophy and karaoke ethos.[3] Karaoke's conquest of France has not been without obstacles, though, since for years lawyers, manufacturers, bar owners, journalists, authors and others have kept very much alive the debate on the connection between authors' copyright and karaoke reproduction. During the last few years, however, the argument seems to have swung in favour of the consumers and the manufacturers of karaoke products.[4]

The resounding success of the television programme 'Star Academy', described by a French journalist as 'improved karaoke' (*karaoké amélioré*), contributed to the consolidation of karaoke in France and Belgium. Its format, combining a talent show with a love story, has enjoyed unprecedented popularity throughout Europe, from Italy to Greece and Spain. Its promise of fame and happiness has prompted many to seek out the nearest karaoke bar to try out their singing talents. Belgian and French karaoke bars are now filled not only with occasional punters, but also with a great number of serious, committed singers. Singing contests with juries and prizes in the spirit of the Olympics abound.[5] In 2002 the Liège piano-bar La Notte, described by Alain Anciaux as a 'little song conservatoire' (*petit conservatoire de la chanson*), had a catalogue of more than three thousand karaoke titles in English and about four thousand titles in French. Every Tuesday and Wednesday, young people would try out specific types of repertoire under the 'musical direction' of the owner.[6]

In the lively Parisian neighbourhood of the Marais, where fancy design bars nestle side by side with smelly felafel shops and Jewish cultural centres, it is not difficult to find big screens and karaoke machines. One particularly exciting 'Karaoke Night Fever', aimed especially at a gay audience, is presented by Les Tampax Samourais, who invite everyone to grab the mike and become rock stars.

Several karaoke venues are listed in the capital's *Pariscope* and *Officiel des Spectacles*. Venues such as the very central L'Annexe or Café Paris-Halles offer a tantalizing mixture of food and karaoke. One venue in Montparnasse, Alexia Metal City, tempts customers with the slogan 'No longer do you have to choose between party and food', and offers a floor show too.[7] Outside Paris, karaoke venues are ever more popular, serving the complete deal of food, song and alcohol on the menu. In Montpellier, locals and tourists alike enjoy going to the Bougalou Café, which hosts a constant stream of parties, stag nights and wedding receptions in a jolly

atmosphere enhanced by wonderful cocktails. Campsites in the south of France, effectively budget beach resorts with all the conveniences of a small village, including shops, restaurants and bars, swimming pools, tennis courts, areas for pétanque and supervised children's activities, offer free nightly entertainment including both musical skits and karaoke.[8]

Holiday camp hosts and aspiring television stars are among the driving forces behind karaoke's success in Europe. In the early 1990s the little-known Rosario Fiorello, once a holiday camp host but now one of Italy's most popular entertainers, made a huge success out of a television programme called simply 'Karaoke'. The shows functioned as a singing contest, with the same selection of songs, changing from night to night, performed by the various contestants. Every show was held in a new location, usually the main piazza of a small town or village, with the live

audience choosing the winner through their wild cheering. During its
first series (1992–3) the programme visited more than 90 different places
and was watched by an average of 3 million viewers per night. The second
series of 'Karaoke' enjoyed an even bigger audience share (20 per cent),
reaching 5.5 million viewers. To celebrate its success, all the contestants
on the last show of the second series, which was staged in Rome, were all
well-known figures, including professional singers and actors and even
the city's mayor.

In a nation that keenly cultivates its double passion for public singing
and televised singing contests, as shown by the daily fare, from song to
opera, on offer throughout the peninsula, and by the 20 million viewers
who tune in to the Festival della canzone di Sanremo, an annual pop song
competition, the formula of karaoke was bound to be a winner. And yet,
some fifteen years later, in the context of a rising scandal over professionals taking part in so-called 'reality TV' shows, Fiorello confessed that
karaoke was a fix. By way of an apology, he admitted that, since the producers could not take the risk that there might be five or six contestants
singing the wrong notes (*steccare*) in the course of a single show, they hired

piano-bar singers or other professionals. He claimed that he did not know about the set up at the time, but not many people seem to believe him.[9]

The popular success of karaoke sparked countless polemics and venomous comments in Italy's fractious media, especially among political commentators. The programme went out nightly on Italia 1, one of the three private television channels belonging to the growing media empire of Silvio Berlusconi, who founded his own Forza Italia party in 1993 and was elected Italy's Prime Minister by April 1994: 'Probably because of its association with TV, and especially with Berlusconi's TV, which is regarded as reactionary and consolatory, karaoke has had a right-wing reputation in Italy since its beginning.'[10]

Certainly Berlusconi has embraced karaoke wholeheartedly and incorporated it into his political practices. Recalling the Prime Minister's boisterous entrance into the political arena, Giampaolo Pansa, one of Italy's most authoritative journalists and social commentators, wrote:

> That was a crazy Sunday. The speech lasted for one hour . . . He had only one objective: to present himself as the Demiurge of the Second Republic, the new man of the Italian miracle . . . At the end, loudspeakers played the party's song at maximum volume. 'Let's sing together', shouted Berlusconi pointing at the big screen behind him where the lyrics were rolling down. They all sang at the top of their voices, crying, laughing.[11]

More than ten years on, Berlusconi remains faithful to karaoke. At the last party congress, both the Italian anthem and the party's eponymous song 'Forza Italia' ('Go, Italy!') were sung karaoke-style. One commentator wryly remarked that this was 'a karaoke congress', extending the metaphor to cover the sense of repetition and the poor imitation of earlier discussions she experienced.[12] Other observers made the association between Berlusconi's raise to power and the growing success of karaoke more or less explicit. Some concerned philosophers and political scientists have even analysed the future that might befall the Left in Italy when faced with such dreadful 'karaoke times'.

Karaoke's success in Italy has also benefited Berlusconi in other ways. For instance, the BBC's pop charts programme 'Top of the Pops', distributed in Italy by Berlusconi's channel Italia 1, has enjoyed millions of viewers. On the back of that success, an interactive application was launched that enabled viewers to access a karaoke version of the tracks in the charts, view video clips of the songs and watch special backstage interviews with the artists. Ringtones of the songs could be downloaded to Italian mobile phones, and more than 80,000 downloads were made between February and April 2004.[13]

There is more to karaoke in Italy, however, than politics and television. As in many other European countries, karaoke can be found in bars and nightclubs, resorts and holiday camps. At the first Italian karaoke bar, Bella lì, which opened in Milan in 1992, you could make a copy of the video cassette recorded during your performance and take it home to show to your friends. Today, hundreds of Italian bars and nightclubs have karaoke evenings at least once a week. From expensive Milanese lounge bars to shady drinking holes in the Genoese docks, karaoke machines are everywhere. Right from its introduction, Italian singers have shown a preference for songs in Italian by Italian composers, usually those popularized

Karaoke wedding, Villa Habana, Italy.

by the Sanremo song contest.[14] Not everyone seems to like this state of
affairs, though, as a sceptical karaoke neophyte's funny, but disconsolate,
account of a karaoke night in Genoa demonstrates:

If you are imaging a sleek sushi bar with a stellar sound-system, interesting tunes, great fun and young people . . . you are miles away from
it. The place is a squalid little hole on the Corso Italia promenade in
Genoa. It may have been chic back in the 1960s but now feels like a
setting for a satirical comedy on the Italian petty bourgeoisie. It is
populated by sad souls. The guy who deals with the machine is a little man dressed in line with the nautical theme of the place, as if he
had just alighted from a yacht in the luxury little village of Portofino.
It was massively boring. Some of the people could sing but most
songs were the same syrupy 'Great Italian Melody' ones and everyone
took themselves so very seriously. At every table were dark sad faces,
of patrons who waited for their turn to sing in order to spread depression and broken hearts among the rest of the crowd.[15]

As in almost every other European country, Italian websites are full of karaoke-related homepages and commercial businesses. Giammarco De Vincentis's homepage (www.cepostaperme.it/cantaconme/; 'there's mail for me/sing with me'), to give just one example, contains hundreds of song lyrics and MIDI files that people can download for free.[16] The music industry has also tried to approach Italians directly to learn their opinions about karaoke. In 2004 the multinational EMI launched on its website the 'EMI music forum' on the subject of karaoke. The relatively few messages deposited in this box were supposed to address the question 'Do you like karaoke? Do you practice it?' A self-described 'dilettante entertainer' wrote enthusiastically: 'I have been doing a little karaoke lately, it drives people crazy'. A young girl confessed that she loves karaoke but prefers to sing in the privacy of her own home, using the VanBasko software. Others responded by admitting to having the same feelings and using the same software for home karaoke. Some respondents were thoroughly against singing karaoke in public, while others praised owners who offered karaoke evenings in bars and nightclubs. Finally, this being Italy after all, some people complained about the lack of arias from the Italian operatic repertory that could be sung karaoke-style.[17]

If the nights of many adult Italians are filled with songs and singing, karaoke can be a daytime pursuit, too, especially among children and young teenagers. Sales of karaoke machines for private use are increasing, partly because teenagers love to sing with their peers while imitating the moves of their favourite pop stars.[18]

While many do karaoke to imitate, Silvia thinks karaoke represents creativity. She is the ebullient founder, together with Pallina and Natasha, of the *Ciboh* creative collective. Their work is subtle, subversive and often edible ('cibo' means food in Italian), and it playfully pokes fun at received ideas about modern art, clothing, design, and food.

After she graduated from the Academy of Arts in Milan, Silvia went to live in Japan, where she learned about traditional paper-making techniques and discovered sweet fizzy drinks, *kawaii* culture and, of course, karaoke:

Karaoke is great. I have always wanted to be the protagonist of a show. I love the stage and the microphone, and the fact that everyone is watching me. In Japan you can rent a karaoke box and have fun with your friends, but in the US it is much better, you are on the stage, you are holding a microphone and everyone listens to you, it's like the real thing!

With a mischievous smile, she continues, 'I always sing the most difficult songs, even if I don't have much of a voice. I love to cry out the most passionate lyrics, the most difficult tunes.'[19]

The other *Ciboh* girls are also passionate about karaoke, especially Pallina, who is known among her friends as *la regina del karaoke* ('the queen of karaoke') and owns the home karaoke unit and brightly coloured microphones the *Ciboh* make great use of. Silvia insists on performing dance routines to her own choreography when she sings her favourite pop tunes on stage. She does not find her limited English much of a problem, but makes up the words as she sings along.

For Silvia, karaoke is not merely 'fun': it represents freedom of expression and creativity – and constant surprises. When travelling, the *Ciboh* never miss an opportunity to have fun at a karaoke venue. Recently they found a small bar in Manhattan where, to spice things up, drinks were on offer to clients who agreed to take off some of their clothes while singing on the small stage. An entire bottle was up for grabs for anyone who dared to undress completely. Wow! Naked karaoke! 'When I turned', says Silvia with a contented smile, 'he was there, stark naked, still singing wildly in the middle of the stage with his white socks on.' She quickly reached for her camera.

Naked karaoke in New York.

Perhaps next time Silvia will not have to go as far as New York to find naked karaoke, but only head south to Rocce Bianche, the wonderful and romantic gay nude beach in Taormina, Sicily. Beach resorts and holiday camps are indeed popular venues for karaoke in Italy. From the exclusive, adult-only Club Med near Otranto in Apulia to the family-orientated Sardinian camping sites, anyone who visits the Italian seaside is likely to experience karaoke. And karaoke is not only to be found in French or Italian summer resorts, but all around the Mediterranean coast and across its islands, from the smallest Greek isle to clubbing-crazy Ibiza.[20]

Karaoke thrives in northern Europe, too. In 2004 Finland, which has a population of about 5.5 million inhabitants, was reported to have roughly two thousand karaoke venues, many of which have a daily karaoke event. In the Helsinki region one can find somewhere open at any time from 9 am to 4 am. During the winter the ski resorts of Lapland resound to karaoke singing, as do the cruise ships that sail between Finland, Sweden and Estonia. In recent years several karaoke championships have been held to celebrate the European passion for karaoke. In 2004 alone there were the Finnish Karaoke Championship, the FinBaltic Karaoke Contest, which attracted

Birthday party karaoke in Helsinki.

more than nine thousand competitors from Sweden, Estonia, Latvia, Lithuania and Finland, and, the most ambitious of all, the Karaoke World Championship.[21] The last of these has been held annually, since 2002, in Heinola, a small town in southern Finland. The competition is not for professional singers but is open to amateurs who are interested in karaoke singing. There are separate competitions for men and women, but otherwise all ages compete on equal terms: anyone over sixteen years of age is allowed to enter. Competitors have a free choice of language and are allowed to bring their own karaoke backgrounds for their songs: only original DVDS and Laserdiscs are allowed. Each contestant should have five different songs, none of which may exceed three minutes in length. The ten finalists (five women and five men), chosen on the reactions of the audience and judges to the overall performances, each receive an award, and the two winners of the men's and women's finals are declared World Champions of Karaoke.[22] Finland is home to several other world championships and large-scale popular events, including the World

Sauna Championship, already held for the seventh time. One that attracts international notice, and some bewilderment, is the annual Wife-Carrying World Championship held in Sonkajärvi since 1992, which is claimed to be charged with

> competitive spirit and is renowned for its warm and humorous atmosphere . . . The wife to be carried may be your own, the neighbour's or you may have found her further afield . . . The minimum weight of the wife to be carried is 49 kilos. If it is less than 49 kilos, the wife will be burdened with such a heavy rucksack that the total weight to be carried is 49 kilos. If a contestant drops his wife, that couple will be fined 15 seconds per drop.[23]

Artists and local musicians have their own share in adding to public enjoyment at Sonkajärvi, since alongside the wife-carrying sporting competition there is also time for music and entertainment, with bands playing music in the arena, wife-carrying dances and wife-carrying karaoke.

From wild championships in Finland to television contests and summer camps, European karaoke has several, seemingly contradictory, faces. The proliferation of different practices and activities, however, points to a thorough appropriation of karaoke by Europeans. Europe has embraced karaoke. Even the European Union has given it a stamp of official approval. For the closing event of the 2003 Comenius Week, which is intended to promote cooperation in education and training throughout the European Community, the leaders of the various workshop groups composed what the EC's official website describes as 'a very original song about friendship, peace and harmony in Europe'. During the week the pupils underwent a complete karaoke induction workshop: 'To help the pupils with the words, the lyrics were projected on a big screen. The first step was to listen to the music, based on a Spanish pop song . . . Some pupils were invited to record parts of the song in their own language.'[24] The results were integrated into a karaoke song that now features on the Comenius Week CD-ROM sent to schools throughout Europe after the event.

Karaoke in Brazil: The Nikkeijin Story

'*Oi japonês!*' ('Hei, Japanese!'). There can be very few Japanese-Brazilians – the largest community of Japanese descent (*Nikkeijin*, literally 'sun line people') outside Japan – who have not been addressed in this way as they go about their daily lives. 'Because of our faces, we can't deny that we are japonês even if we wanted to, we are reminded of this whenever we walk down the street.'[1] Being a *japonês* in today's Brazil, however, does not necessarily carry the array of negative connotations and social stigmas usually associated with being identified as a 'minority'; on the contrary, a host of positive stereotypes are associated with being one. Japanese-Brazilians are often regarded as hard-working, responsible, trustworthy and clever, as well as timid and reserved, all characteristics that are attributed a positive value by both majority Brazilians and minority Japanese-Brazilians.

Japanese immigrants first arrived in Brazil in 1908 following negotiations between the government of the state of São Paulo, which was much in need of agricultural workers on its coffee, cotton and sugar plantations, and private Japanese emigration companies operating with the support of the Meiji regime to help to contain serious rural population pressures. With the accession of the Taisho emperor in 1912, Japanese emigration to Brazil rose again. During the post-war period Japanese migrants started to move towards the cities where many now reside, including in São Paulo. More than 1.2 million people in Brazil are ethnically identified as Japanese, though the majority of Nikkei Brazilians would probably regard themselves as assimilated both culturally and socially. The prestige associated with 'Japaneseness' in Brazilian society, compounded with the persistence of ethnic labelling and, in some cases, of outward discrimination, has contributed to the continuity of practices perceived as distinctively Japanese. There are, for example, numerous active associations and clubs running a multitude of 'ethnic activities' and events ranging from festivals to theatre, from language courses to dance and sporting events, from the 'Miss Nikkei' beauty pageant to karaoke contests. Japanese migrants to Brazil have generally been regarded as economically successful. Statistics on socio-economic status and educational achievements, for instance, appear significantly higher than those for the rest of the Brazilian population, which is thought to have contributed to the relative popularity of Japanese cultural practices, including cuisine, manga and karaoke, among Brazilians of non-Japanese descent. 'It's amazing how many Brazilians want to learn Japanese', a Japanese-Brazilian university student told a researcher. It has no practical value for them, he admitted, but 'they just do it out of personal interest in Japanese culture.' Some of them even learn to sing Japanese songs in order to take part in the numerous karaoke contests organized by the Japanese-Brazilian community.[2]

Until the late 1970s the karaoke scene in Brazil was limited to some thirty bars, with a predominantly male clientele, in the São Paulo area. In the 1980s, however, karaoke spread widely to include singers who were not necessarily drunk, male or even adult'.[3] The karaoke singing contest was born. Isabel-Cristina Leme, although not a Nikkei by birth or marriage, simply loves to sing Japanese songs. In an interview with the *Jornal Nippo-Brasil* she explained how she was hooked by Japanese music as a teenager when watching the 'Japan Pop Show' on television. She is now so proficient that she can take part in such top-level karaoke competitions as the eleventh annual Concurso de Karaokê do Estado de São Paulo. The traffic of songs and singers between Japan and Brazil has a fairly long history. In 1998, for example, the very popular television programme 'NHK Amateur Singing Contest' was staged in São Paulo, the first occasion in its long history the show had left Japan. The special edition commemorated the ninetieth anniversary of the first Japanese emigrants to Brazil. The next year further editions of the show were broadcast from other capitals of the

'Japanese Diaspora': Lima, Hawai'i, Buenos Aires, San Francisco and Beijing. Many of today's favourite karaoke songs, among both Japanese and Brazilian singers, originally featured in television programmes, including the highly popular 'Red & White Year-end Song Festival'.[4] In recent years Brazilian karaoke singers of Japanese descent have even started taking part, with some success, in the Nihon Amateur Kaoyu Sai Grand Prix Taikai and other karaoke competitions in Japan.

In the Brazilian Nikkei world *Karaokê* is complex and highly stratified. Many Nikkei associations invite professional singers and music teachers to give karaoke instruction classes. In 1995 there were between 120 and 150 clubs of this type in São Paulo alone.[5] *Karaokê* contests are highly organized affairs with hundreds of participants, large audiences paying entrance fees, sizeable monetary prizes and media coverage. Every contest is usually overseen by one president (occasionally there are also honorary presidents), one or two vice-presidents, one or two general coordinators and vice coordinators. In addition there is a jury, which also has a president, a vice-president and so on, and is often composed of several groups of jurors. The participants are divided into many different categories, according to age, skills and musical genre. Some associations, such as the União Paulista de Karaokê (Karaoke Union of São Paulo), have been formed with the precise aim of standardizing the criteria for assessing a singer's performance in each contest and his/her consequent profile.

A major event such as the 2002 All-Brazilian Karaoke Championship might be divided into numerous categories to cater for the range of experience and ages of those taking part. The *veterano* category includes those over the age of 41, and is further divided into three sub-categories; *adulto* covers those aged between 18 and 40; and *juvenil* is for teenagers, 14–17. Those in the child categories of *doyo* (school song singers) and *tibiko* (child imitator) must be no more than 13 – and some can be less than 6 years old. The singers are also classified on the basis of their achievements. Using a ranking system similar to that traditionally employed for Japanese martial arts, in order to get a better ranking, one must regularly take part in contests organized by the official karaoke associations. Japanese-Brazilians are so proud of their organization of the karaoke scene that they think it is even 'more advanced' than the Japanese one.[6]

By 2002, when she was just seventeen years old, Lilian Tangoda had already won the popular jury prize at the Concurso Brasileiro da Canção Japonesa and the semi-legal Brazilian betting agencies were already considering her one of the potential winners of the eighteenth annual contest before it had even started. In an interview she gave to the *Jornal Nippo-Brazil*, she claimed to have started training when she was just two months old, and devoted her victory to her parents, who were everything to her. Without them she would never have managed to train so hard.

Nikkeijin karaoke: Lilian Tangoda, a winner of the Brasilerao.

While in Brazil karaoke and other 'Japanese' practices represent a way for Nikkei Brazilians to assert their ethnic identity, things are quite different in Japan. According to the *Wall Street Journal*, between 1983 and 1998 about 200,000 of the estimated 1.2 million ethnic Japanese in the São Paulo area of Brazil moved to Japan.[7] There, however, the *Nikkeijin* face various forms of discrimination and ostracism. While regarded as *japonês* in Brazil, in Japan they are definitely considered and treated as *gaijin* or 'foreigners'. One Nikkei worker summarized his condition thus: 'I am a foreigner. My hair is long; I have a beard; I gesticulate; my *meishi* [name card] is written in *katakana*. There is no doubt I am a foreigner who lives in Japan.'[8] Although Japanese legislation does in theory permit naturalization, between 1952 and 1992 only 221,000 foreigners became naturalized Japanese, an average of only 5,500 per year. Many Nikkei Brazilians work in Japan with special visas issued by the Ministry of Labour to Japanese-descended foreigners. If, however, the Japanese government and businesses initially welcomed *Nikkeijin* as a preferred alternative to foreign migrants who were not 'ethnically' Japanese, the onset of recession led some Japanese to label Brazilian workers of Japanese ascent as irresponsible and untrustworthy. As brokered workers, *Nikkeijin* often have little incentive to stay loyal to their employers. The first to be laid off during economic downturns, and more or less openly ostracized, they have learned to look out for themselves. Not surprisingly, *Nikkeijin* living in Japan sometimes become more 'Brazilian', taking to samba dance and organizing substitutes for carnival. Some of them even feel that they must do something for their unwelcoming hosts: 'We Brazilian *Nikkeijin* are here to liven up Japan because it is a half-dead country'.[9]

As for karaoke, if the members of the Brazilian Nikkei community love to sing Japanese songs, in Japan, by contrast, they give heartfelt renditions of Brazilian songs. Just over 10 per cent of the population of the city of Oizumi in Gunma prefecture is made up of foreigners – a percentage even higher than that of certain areas of Tokyo. Most of these are Brazilians of Japanese descent, and the findings of a team from Connecticut College offer interesting glimpses of Nikkei life in Japan. During the weekends, Oizumi fills up with young *Nikkeijin* from all over Japan, who meet in nightclubs like ATR and Choppe Video to dance samba and sing karaoke. According to one reveller at ATR, 'Oizumi is a great place to come for the weekend. When I am here I feel like I am back in Brazil. I can share memories and enjoy myself with my kind of people.' Summarizing her findings, one researcher writes:

> I found that karaoke was a popular activity amongst the clubs much like in Brazil but the difference is that the Nikkei living in Brazil sing to Japanese lyrics while those in Oizumi sing to Brazilian lyrics. When they are in Brazil they feel like Japan is their home while in Japan they feel that Brazil is their home.[10]

Karaoke, the new sport in Brazil: Mike enjoys a karaoke revolution.

These findings are not dissimilar from those of Casey Lum with regard to Chinese-Americans, for whom karaoke 'provides the social and symbolic structure for people to create, maintain, and transform social realities and meanings that are true and significant to them.'[11]

Karaoke Revolution:
Karaoke Technologies

'A Karaoke in Every Home'

In 1992 an *International Herald Tribune* article, provokingly titled 'Now, a Karaoke in Every Home?', chronicled the increasing production and popularity of karaoke technology for domestic use. The author, not much of a karaoke fan himself, sardonically commented that karaoke was 'not sophisticated stuff' and that karaoke machines were 'basically the high-tech descendants of Mr Microphone, a device hawked years ago in the middle of the night on American cable TV, along with other necessities, such as the Garden Weasel, the Popeet Pocket Fisherman and the "amazing Ginsu knives".'[1] Readers from the US may have found the reference to Mr Microphone (a device consisting of a microphone containing an AM transmitter that enabled one's voice to be heard over the radio. It enjoyed some popularity in the 1970s and '80s thanks especially to a successful, if tasteless, advertisement campaign) highly amusing, and yet the comparison is rather far-fetched. Even if karaoke generally relies on pre-existing technologies, and basic microphone technology has indeed been around for well over a century, the market for new karaoke machines and karaoke-related gadgets does not show any sign of becoming saturated. On the contrary, new and more sophisticated products emerge every day and consumers are spoilt for choice.

At the beginning of the twenty-first century, Japan is no longer the only place where karaoke-related technology is enjoying widespread success. The rest of Asia, Europe and North America are also witnessing an explosion in the use of such gadgetry. As a CNN reporter discovered with a touch of disbelief, 'Karaoke has warbled its way into the American living room.'[2]

To a certain extent, technological innovation has been at the very heart of the karaoke phenomenon since the invention of the 8-Juke machine in the 1970s. Developments in the quality of the audio and visual signals, as well as improvements in user-friendliness and accessibility, have always been key requirements for manufacturers and users alike. Soon after the commercial introduction of the first machines, which were basically reel-to-reel tape players, these were replaced by cassette tapes, and then by audiocassettes, videotapes, CDs, laser discs, CDGs (CD plus graphics) and, eventually, by cable karaoke (also known as 'telecom karaoke' or 'online karaoke'). Indeed, the invention of video karaoke, which had the double advantage of showing the lyrics on screen and of capturing the audience's attention through the use of images, represented a crucial step forward. As the then president of the Karaoke International Singalong Association put it: 'With the lyrics on TV, the whole room gets to watch, and they get sucked into the experience.'[3]

When karaoke machines first hit the global market they were still comparatively expensive. In 1982, however, Pioneer introduced laser karaoke technology, and soon after the first laser disc machine for domestic use appeared on the commercial market. It took the Japanese market by storm. Unlike cassette tapes and videocassettes, which had to follow a preset order, this technology provided the enormous advantage of granting random access to the songs.

During the 1990s online technology further revolutionized karaoke in Japan. Using karaoke-on-demand, thousands of songs can be transmitted digitally over telephone wires to clubs and homes, where they are stored on computer hard disks or CD-ROMs for easy replay. Taito Corporation introduced the X-55 service in 1995. Its huge selection of songs attracted an even larger number of subscribers, especially among the young. Pioneer, Sega Enterprise, Clarion and other manufacturers raced to join the market. By the end of 1996, 25 per cent of karaoke systems in Japan were online.

Another major innovation was introduced in 1996 when Timeware Corporation launched a virtual karaoke system that allows singers to select a virtual concert hall in which they would like to sing. Using a special mixer, data processing sound board and power amps, such a system can reproduce the acoustic characteristics of famous concert halls. Singers can also design a virtual space to suit their voice. The experience can be made even more real by incorporating other electronic instruments and videos.[4]

In less than twenty years constant innovation and careful marketing strategies have transformed karaoke into a global technology. By the early 1990s British manufacturers including Goodmans and Arbiter, as well as several companies in Hong Kong and other South-east Asian countries, were marketing their own brands of karaoke machines: the Goodmans Boogie Box and Arbiter K5900 sold in huge numbers leading up to Christmas 1991.[5]

In the early 1990s Pioneer was still the undisputed leader in karaoke manufacturing, but it was already losing its supremacy by the end of that decade. As karaoke became a global commodity, cultural differences became an issue for suppliers. Pioneer tried to introduce the concept of the karaoke box to the United States, but it failed. Living in larger houses than their Asian counterparts, many Americans tend to socialize at home, and house parties are what they like to do. As a result home units came to dominate the karaoke market. One of the favourite models was the relatively inexpensive Sony CDP-K1, which is basically a CD player with karaoke functions and two microphones for dubbing over the vocal lines. The CDP-K1 also features a digital echo circuit and a user-adjustable pitch control, allowing a singer's notes to be ratcheted up or down an octave. The device was widely popular among those whose desire to perform far exceeded their ability.

Meanwhile, the Hong Kong company vtech began to target the European market with battery-operated, portable karaoke for kids, sold as a learning tool aimed at improving children's IQ by teaching them to make music and sing from a very early age. The idea was immediately taken up by other toy companies worldwide and children's karaoke machines were the hottest property at the New York's Toy Fair trade show in 2002. After

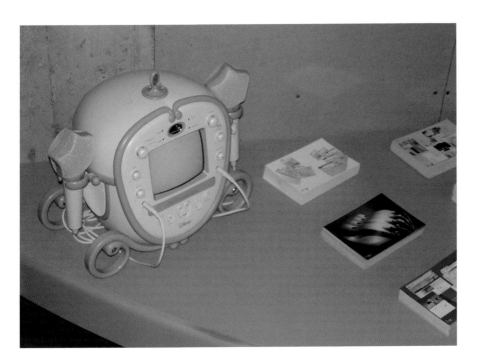

A cinderella karaoke set.

the initial success of its DJ Jazz Jam, which came on the market in 2000, VTech exhibited the improved DJ Karaoke Studio model, a comprehensive little music machine for the North American market, suitable for children aged three and older, with a working microphone, a one-octave keyboard and 24 preset tunes.

For older children Toymax put out the more sophisticated VJ Starz Karaoke Music Studio, a tiny, stylish unit with a built-in video camera that can be hooked up to a television set so that one can watch oneself on the screen while performing. It also allows singers to tape their own performances using a videocassette recorder.[6]

In recent years software companies have sought to explore the economic potential of karaoke with educational products aimed at children and young adults. For a mere $30, for example, American parents can now enhance their children's potential literacy skills through the Windows software 'Jumpstart Reading with Karaoke', which allegedly helps children learn to read by performing special karaoke songs using the microphone included in the package. Children are asked to unlock new karaoke songs by playing learning games that teach them the words found in the songs. In one such game users have to sort words into 'talking garbage cans' by identifying each word's initial sound. In another, they must put alphabet-adorned boxes into a delivery truck in a specific order so as to spell a word; once in the truck the word is highlighted and the children are asked to utter it.[7] The software ingeniously incorporates children's voices into the learning process by having them speak or sing into a microphone. One can only wonder if all these highly literate baby prodigies will grow up to become 'karaoke addicts'!

Karaoke microphones: between toys and technological prostheses

Back in the 1920s and '30s the introduction of the microphone contributed to the emergence and spread of new vocal styles and singing techniques. As Paula Lockheart has observed, early microphone singing style can be regarded as 'the embodiment of the American populist ideal of the time', creating a sound that may be described as democratic, natural, untrained and close to everyday conversational speech, at least when set against the classical European tradition of vocal delivery.[8] Today, the world of karaoke singing seems to mirror some of the populist elements introduced to professional American singing by the advent of microphones and electric recording. Can everyone sing with a microphone? Perhaps, provided it is a karaoke Magic Mic.

For those who sing at karaoke venues, the microphone exudes a special aura. Every karaoke culture the world over develops its own traditions and specific concerns about the technological tool of the karaoke singer's trade. Mastery of a microphone's technical characteristics, the angle and distance it should be held from the mouth, the vocal effects that can be achieved – such knowledge is an essential requirement for any aspiring karaoke singer. Yet there are also taboos specific to individual cultures, including many things one should never do, such as holding the mike in two hands instead of one or even raising one's little finger while holding it. Japanese karaoke gurus tend to be fairly prescriptive about the dos and don'ts of microphone etiquette. Even if things may seem superficially more relaxed in Europe, there is still common agreement on good and bad ways to deal with hand-held microphones, especially with regards to their ostensibly phallic shape. In the experience of the anthropologist and world karaoke practitioner Alain Anciaux, there are many microphone 'syndromes' in the karaoke world. Some people hold a microphone as if it were dirty, using just the tips of their fingers; others give the impression of being afraid of catching germs – what he calls 'germicrophobia' – and clean it each time before singing. Others hold it as if it were a flute, moving their fingers as if playing an instrument, or as if it were a penis. In some European countries, and in the usa, letting go of the mike during a performance is deemed worthy of punishment and the culprit has to pay for a round of drinks.[9] Microphones are hit, patted, played, shouted at, loved and feared.

Increasingly more sophisticated devices keep emerging in the ever-expanding world of home karaoke machines, including the 'all-in-one' models (also known as 'Magic Mics'). 'Magic Sing' is a wireless video karaoke microphone unit, and the ivl Karaoke tv star All In One Microphone claims to 'make a crow sound like a canary'. Bringing to aspiring karaoke stars the advanced technology devised to aid professional singers, the tvstar microphone can adjust the key, add reverb, slow the tempo down and even transform a male voice into a female one.[10] Owners of Magic Mics appreciate their unique technical features, which afford them the illusion of sounding like real pop stars. Magic Mics can be programmed to contain thousands of in-built songs in several languages, including Chinese, English and Tagalog, and can be attached to television sets so that people may watch themselves and be watched. Unlike aspiring pop stars in televised singing contests, however, karaoke fans hang on to their hand-held microphones and are not prepared to give them up in favour of any glitzy headset. Microphones are their favourite toys.

A toy is certainly what the E-karamix looks like and is marketed as. A pink microphone vaguely reminiscent of a dildo, the E-karamix was released in Japan in 2004. This device can download songs from the Internet and is even equipped with a terminal so that users without an Internet connection can download songs at any toyshop.[11]

In a world dominated by portable gadgets, whose usefulness is often overstated to disguise their secondary leisure features, Magic Mics, the ultimate portable karaoke machines, are unashamedly ludic. Not surprisingly, they now count as 'standard picnic equipment second only to the portable grill'.[12]

'Everything that is karaoke': karaoke on the Web

In January 1996 Microsoft linked up with Nikkodo, a major karaoke equipment and software company, to launch an online home karaoke service in Japan via the Microsoft network. In the space of a few months Nikkodo supplied more than ten thousand tunes to users. After its initial success, Microsoft turned to the worldwide market. This marked a new era in karaoke technology.

Eatsleepmusic.com, a company incorporated in Ottawa in 1999, was awarded a prize by a local industry group in 2001 for 'changing the way people play' with its Internet karaoke service, providing users with the tools they need to turn any PC into a karaoke machine. Via the Eatsleepmusic network, the company sells computer hardware and even offers singing lessons to millions of users. They also license their applications to other companies, including Canoe and Lycos.[13]

The success of Eatsleepmusic.com is but one example. The last few years have seen an exponential growth of software programs that turn one's home computer into a quasi-karaoke machine. This technology also enables karaoke jockeys (KJS) to load all the necessary material onto their computers' hard drives rather than carry around hundreds of compact discs when hosting a show. The world wide web contains thousands, perhaps hundreds of thousands, of commercial karaoke sites aimed at the growing market of karaoke professionals from, to cite but two examples, www.fiestaKaraoke.com.ar/ in Argentina to www.ozkaraoke.com.au/ in Australia, which presents itself to potential clients thus:

> From karaoke hire systems and shows through to disc and equipment sales, Oz Karaoke has it all. Whether your function is a private party, a large corporate function or you would like a regular professional karaoke show at your venue, Oz Karaoke has a system package to suit. Start building your own karaoke system! From home systems to professional show systems, Oz Karaoke has everything that is karaoke.

The relative ease and speed with which karaoke files can be uploaded and downloaded, even over relatively slow internet connections, has been a contributory factor in turning the world wide web into the largest source of karaoke-related materials and information for fans, practitioners and professionals alike. It has created a veritable global web of karaoke communities. An exploration of the web pages created by karaoke fans the world over reveals that they are passionate about sharing their experiences and, most of all, their own karaoke renditions of famous songs. Could this desire be fuelled by the illusion of singing for an audience of millions?

While homepages explicitly devoted to karaoke are fairly common in North America, the number of European sites is also increasing.[14] In China, Japan and throughout South-east Asia, countless karaoke web pages have been set up for fans to share tips, buy accessories, sing online or comment about the latest karaoke success.

Some webmasters address the particular necessities of their fellow local practitioners. The fairly provincial world of Italian karaoke contains a webpage maintained by a certain Wainer Valido.[15] With the motto 'Canta anche tu con Wainer Valido' ('Sing along with Wainer Valido'), Mr Valido creatively approaches the problem of singing in an unknown foreign tongue. He boldly declares: 'I am always on your side; I want all of you to make a good impression! Is there a foreign song you like to whistle but are not able to sing? Wainer is here to solve all your problems with his "English for everyone".' In an intriguing reversal of the karaoke industry's claim that it can contribute to acquiring linguistic skills, these pages contain the lyrics of some forty

American and British pop tunes presented in Wainer's own peculiar translit-eration system. Here is how Wainer approaches the iconic 'I Will Survive':

I Will Survive

Et ferst ai uos afreid	At first I was afraid
Ai uos petrifaid	I was petrified
Chep zinching au cul never liv	Kept thinking I could never live
Uidaut iu bai mai said	Without you by my side
Badden ai spenso meni naits	But then I spent so many nights
Zinching au iu didmi ruong	thinking how you did me wrong
Enai griu strong	And I grew strong
Enai lernd au tu gheralong	And I learned how to get along
En so ior bek, frommaure speis	and so you're back, from outer space
Ai giastuolchin tu faindiu iir	I just walked in to find you here
. . .	. . .

Karaoke video games

Another by-product of karaoke's widespread popularity is the karaoke video game. Back in the 1980s the Japanese electronic gadgetry producer Bandai, the same firm that gave the world the electronic pet Tamagotchi, produced the amazing peripheral known as Bandai's Karaoke Studio for the most popu-lar video game producer in the world, Nintendo's Family Computer console, also known as Famicom or the Nintendo Entertainment System (NES). Equipped with a microphone, the game employed versions of 1980s Japanese pop hits using the then limited sound capabilities of the Famicom console. The lyrics appeared on the screen, along with tantalizing artwork depicting the songs' themes. The unit itself plugged into the Famicom's cartridge slot and had fifteen tunes built in, but cartridges with additional songs were also sold by Bandai.[16] The game had many structural problems and was not, in the end, very successful, but it did pave the way for the next generation of karaoke video games, namely SingStar Party and Karaoke Revolution.

SingStar Party is a karaoke game that plugs into the famous PlayStation. With the help of two microphones, SingStar enables players to test their skills against the machine. After each round, the performer's execution is evaluated on the basis of pitch, rhythm and volume, and a score is assigned accordingly. The game is already enjoying great success in Britain and other parts of Europe. In a recent article published in the British daily *The Guardian*, Jess Cartner-Morley passes on a witty description of the game as 'the perfect revenge for PlayStation widows everywhere', referring to the addictiveness of PlayStation games, particularly among young men. She admits that the competitive element is a winning feature of SingStar: 'I have been at dinner parties where dessert was discovered forgotten and untouched in the fridge the following morning by a hungover hostess, victim of the eagerness of all concerned to leave the table and get cracking on the serious business of SingStar.' As one of her microphone colleagues enthused, 'it's similar to when computer games first came out, but much more jubilant'.[17]

The maker Konami has created another console game for the PlayStation 2, poignantly named Karaoke Revolution. Using a game play similar to that of Dance Dance Revolution (DDR), a single player sings along with on-screen guidance and receives a score based upon his or her pitch and rhythm. In order to make the world of karaoke come alive in a video game context, the player may choose from eight characters, each of whom has four different outfits. There are also eight different possible settings in which the game may take place, including a house party, a train station, a stadium show and, not surprisingly, the set of an 'American Idol'-type TV show. A backing band can be present. On-screen audiences can boo or cheer wildly accordingly to the singer's skill. Even the microphone comes into the act, leaving white vapour trails on the screen. Karaoke Revolution breaks the song up into chunks of lyrics, one or two lines of a song, for scoring purposes. The more one's song meter fills up during each segment, the more points one receives. A terrible singer will get a 'Lousy' score, but can move on up to 'Poor', 'OK', 'Good', 'Great' and even 'Expert'. In addition to the meter for each segment, there is an overall meter, divided into three sections: red, yellow, and green. After a truly excellent performance the

crowd starts cheering and special effects appear on the screen, including a massive fireworks display. One commentator observed the startling impression such special effects can have upon performers:

> It's funny how such a simple thing as a glowing character and a cheering polygon crowd can affect you. When I was singing the songs, I just started getting into it and I felt bad when my performance was plain awful and got booed off the stage. I would start right over again at the end just to show them what I had.[18]

Generally speaking, in a real karaoke venue one would rarely be humiliated thus, even after a bad performance. Some KJs may make a joke but your friends would surely be there to encourage you. Alas, the virtual reality of video games is not for the faint-hearted.

Karaoke on mobile phones

During the last four or five years mobile phone and mobile content providers throughout the world have nourished the hope that users would take to staring at their handsets and sing. The world's first mobile karaoke service that allowed users to download karaoke songs and display synchronized lyrics and images on their handset was launched in Japan. 'Mobile karaoke customers tend to be 20-something women and middle-aged men', commented Yoshihiro Watanabe, a spokesman for a Nagoya-based firm that offers mobile phone users downloadable karaoke tunes, 'who like to rehearse before heading for the karaoke box.'[19] Recently the service has been widened so that users can send up to four photos, which can be watched while the audio clip is playing. According to a survey, in 2002 Japanese people spent some 80 billion yen (£427 million) on ring tones and mobile karaoke. Downloading karaoke songs costs as much as sending a text message and new songs are released every day. In 2003 the giant mobile phone network Vodaphone Japan launched yet a new service that allowed subscribers to plug their handset into a TV to watch the lyrics on the big screen, while singing into the phone's mouthpiece.[20] Following suit, Singaporeans, Malaysian, Koreans, Americans, and Russian mobile phone users were soon also able to purchase similar services. The mobile content developer First International Digital, for instance, recently launched the first Karaoke service in the US with 50 polyphonic karaoke songs, including songs by popular artists, festive tunes and even patriotic songs. Users can now purchase individual songs for $1.25, or in bundles of three ($3.49) or six ($5.99) units. The karaoke giant Sound Choice released its catalogue of more than 15,000 karaoke tracks for mobile phone users and launched ListenToMeSing, a sort of community that allows karaoke enthusiasts to share their performances with others. As well as sharing song renditions with other members, enthusiasts may send an email link to friends outside the community or allow people to vote and give user feedback on performances.[21]

Karaoke mobiles arrived in Russia in April 2005 and popular songs can already be downloaded to phones as ringtone melodies for the equivalent of 70 cents and $1 per song. Moreover, mobile karaoke will enable budding Russian singers to download a file that will display running lyrics on the phone screen in time to the music. According to a report in the *St Petersburg Times*, the Russian provider INFON hopes to tap into certain social categories such as businessmen and thirty-something women, who currently do not utilize the advanced functions of their new mobile handsets but have, in the industry's jargon, 'high potential'. Alongside pop hits for the youth market, users can download traditional Russian folksongs. 'We have researched entertainment spots around large cities where there is karaoke, asking what melodies were popular', says Tatyana Timofeyeva, a spokeswoman for INFON, 'and it seems that traditional Russian songs have wild success, that's why we have included them.'[22]

Whereas Russian providers decided to pitch their services to an older audience, if only because their exorbitant prices are likely to be beyond the reach of most Russian teens, when the largest Singaporean telecommunication company launched a similar service to its subscribers, its vice president Hui Weng Cheong declared that the service was aimed especially at the young: 'We see mobile karaoke as an entertaining and innovative service that will appeal especially to the young and anyone who loves to sing.' His company, however, also hopes to exploit realms well beyond solipsistic teen fun: 'With the inclusion of some Christmas songs nearer to the festive period, we are confident that the service will be a hit at Christmas gatherings and parties.'[23] His hopes seem to have been not entirely misconceived, at least judging by the presence on the official website for the celebration of Singapore National Day 2005 of several downloadable karaoke songs, including patriotic tunes such as 'Where I belong', 'Home' and 'We can'.[24]

Ever since the appearance of the first machine, karaoke technology has made enormous progress, with new products emerging every day. It is difficult to estimate the profits made by the karaoke industry throughout the world, but in 2002 it earned some $7 billion in Japan alone, no small sum considering that it was a relatively difficult phase for the Japanese economy. One characteristic of the karaoke phenomenon is the constant dialogue between users and manufacturers. Developments in the quality of the audio and visual signals, and improvements designed to make the devices increasingly accessible, are always welcomed by users. As with other audiovisual products, the wide range of social practices associated with karaoke show that there is always great potential for further invention and development.

Epilogue:
Karaoke at the Frontiers

Leaving China, passengers on board the China Southwest Airlines flight into Tibet were shown a safety video on screens above their seats. The video was backed by the usual choice of music: 'My Way'. It's not the most reassuring thing in the world to start a journey to the high plateau of Tibet on a mainland Chinese aircraft with wording echoing one's head: 'And now the end is near,/and so I face the final curtain'.[1]

Perhaps even more alarming for those travellers looking for a 'unique' experience in 'mysterious and exotic' Tibet is that karaoke is as much a local experience there as it is in China. According to Vivienne Adams, an anthropologist who has conducted fieldwork in Lhasa, 'on nearly every third or fourth street in much of downtown Lhasa one finds a karaoke bar'.[2] Many observers claim that China is swamping Tibetan culture in a number of ways, including ruthless modernization. Office and apartment blocks covered in glaringly coloured tiles, ubiquitous throughout China, known as 'toilet-style' buildings, have also sprouted around Lhasa. The rhythmic pulses of pop music from discos and karaoke bars throb in the shadow of the Potala, the Dalai Lama's former residence. Many pro-Tibet activists have accused China of conducting an 'undercover war' against Tibetan Buddhism. Journalistic reports of this kind often juxtapose places of prayer with karaoke bars:

> Closely watched by security forces and surveillance cameras, dark-robed pilgrims prostrate and turn brass prayer wheels as they circle

the temple. Tibetan children and elderly beggars receive a few coins or barley kernels from worshippers and share their alms with monks, or lamas who chant prayers for the liberation of man. Nearby, new bars, mahjong parlors, and Karaoke halls line Beijing Avenue, the main street that bisects the capital.[3]

On 20 January 1996 the Xinhua News Agency reported that Hainan Province, a tropical island and tax paradise located in the South China Sea, was sponsoring the construction of a hydroelectric power station in Dingqing County, in north-east Tibet, and that the station was already benefitting local people. 'Now residents in Dingqing County have electric lights, colour television sets, electric stoves, even karaoke machines,' allegedly declared Zhalha Gongbu, Magistrate of Dingqing County. While it may be true that the Chinese government banks on such strategies to take the steam out of Tibetan nationalism, some Tibetans have indeed embraced aspects of Chinese modernization, including its entertainment industry, as Vivienne Adams notes, 'For many Lhasa Tibetans karaoke is a significant symbol of modernity'.

Nowadays there are two types of karaoke venues in Lhasa: karaoke 'disco style' and karaoke bars that double as brothels. Karaoke discos provide fairly innocent fun for young and occasionally middle-aged moneyed Tibetan and Chinese patrons. Adams records that women arrive at these bars in groups of two or more, 'dressed in Western-style clothes or, less commonly, in traditional *chupas* (long dresses), silk blouses, wool blazers, high heels, tight-fitting pullovers, hair clips, perfume, short dresses, nylons.' Men also arrive in groups and all dressed up. They rarely sit or dance with the women. Occasionally someone volunteers to sing a tune: 'some men stay at their table and serenade each other with the popular song of the day – love songs – passing the microphone all the way around the table so that everyone has a chance for a chorus line or two of their own, punctuated by long gulps of beer.' Sometimes there are also 'dance shows' where local singers imitate the routines from (usually American) pop song videos while lip-synching the lyrics. The karaoke brothels range from very small and incredibly cheap establishments to larger and more expensive ones. Both Tibetan and Chinese women work as prostitutes in these brothels, where dancing and singing karaoke are part of the preliminaries between the women and their clients.[4] Tibet, the mystical Buddhist land, the 'land of snow', that bastion of the western Orientalist vision of otherness and the frontier, is now truly a 'karaoke land'.

If karaoke is now a symbol of 'modernity' in Tibet, karaoke TVs have also become a focal point at the Sunday market in Kashgar, where multitudes of locals and travellers alike gather in front of them. Situated on the famous Silk Road that fired the Orientalist imagination, at the crossroad between Xinjiang, Pakistan and central Asia, this 'Mother of All Bazaars' is perhaps one of the most exotic and colourful places on earth. Writing in 2003, Pepe Escobar vividly describes the atmosphere in Kashgar that still evokes Marco Polo's *Travels*:

> A monumental traffic jam of donkey carts coils around the muddy borders of the Tuman River – trespassed by horses, Bactrian camels, acres of melancholic sheep and elders brandishing sickles and testing horseshoes, saddles and whips. Sandy alleys bear the conspicuous accumulation of carpets from Hotan, mountains of spices, laminated dowry boxes, bits and pieces of dead animals, very much alive chickens and ducks, the famous Yengisar knives, hats in all shapes and colors, pots and pans, fruits, vegetables, riding boots, prehistoric transistor radios, Pakistani silk stockings, any imaginable agricultural tool hand-made from wood or steel, and the usual paraphernalia of items available in any self-respecting Oriental *souk*. The food is delicious – from bread sprinkled with poppy or sesame seeds to *lahgman* – noodles topped with mutton and vegetables; from *jiger* (liver) kebab to *girde nan* – Uighur bagels.[5]

For anyone who has been to Kashgar, the weekly Sunday market is truly unforgettable. Pepe calls it an 'anthropological delirium', with thousands of villagers and travellers converging on the bazaar.

Alongside arrays of goods, spices, food, animals and people, and the local barbers waving their long sharp knives, people simply love gathering to sing along, their eyes fixed upon karaoke TVs. The characters showing on the screen are all Uighur men with long, pointed beards, decorated hats, dark cloaks and black boots, and women wearing multi-coloured scarves. The language, of course, is Uighur. The music, still on audio cassettes, is *gecekondu arabesk,* Turkish pop.

For centuries music and dance have been central to the life of Uighur people. To this day, most young Uighurs refuse to listen to Chinese pop in protest against China's colonization. Instead they listen to the pungent guitar sounds of Akbar Kahriman and to Turkish pop stars, whose songs are now being sold as karaoke VCDs or CDs and are played loudly on the streets all the way from Urumqi to Kashgar. While Islam has been a powerful means of expressing their distress, open-air karaoke TVs bring them joy and music. They have become an alternative venue to the mosque as somewhere that young Uighurs can meet to have fun and feel united.

Turkish pop karaoke is also widespread at other crossroads throughout central Asia. From Tashkent to Uzbekistan, the once famed Silk Road is now dotted with karaoke places, kebab joints and souvenir stalls. To the modern traveller, the ancient Silk Road is quickly turning into the 'Karaoke Road'.

The end? Or a new beginning?

From Japan and South-east Asia to Europe, North America and central Asia, the karaoke story just goes on and on, seemingly without end. Yet, as we have been told, every story has an ending, at least when one is writing a book. So to close our story we sought to find out about what is arguably the most closed country in the world (at least to western eyes): North Korea.

In 2001 North Korea, which had been heavily dependent on foreign aid since 1995, underwent a major food crisis. Due to power shortages its industries and agriculture, already crippled, were literally collapsing. South Koreans organizations, both private and religious, were most solicitous and generous in their donations.

In January of that year the Chinese-registered freighter *Mingri* left the southern port of Inchon heading for the northern city of Nanpo. The boat carried some $900,000 worth of aid. The aid package consisted of 120 goats and 60 tonnes of fodder, 17,000 sets of underwear, 120 tonnes of flour, 45,500 bottles of cooking oil, 325 boxes of winter garments, 2,562 boxes of stationery and 10 karaoke machines. Aid organizers said that the machines, complete with some 4,000 western and South Korean pop songs, were to be installed at a youth recreational and cultural centre in Pyonyang and would 'contribute to inter-Korean reconciliation'.[6]

After nearly fifty years of conflict, would karaoke finally be able to bring about harmony and reconciliation? Perhaps once North Koreans have learnt those 4,000 western and South Korean pop songs by heart, there will be a new prospect for world peace. Or perhaps not.

Select List of Karaoke Venues Worldwide

EUROPE

LONDON

Lucky Voice Private Karaoke
52 Poland Street, w1
tel. 020 7439 3660
www.luckyvoice.co.uk/
Tokyo-style karaoke box, with state-of-
the-art technology and more than 4,999
songs to choose from. Luxuriously
appointed individual suites cost about
£50 per hour to hire. Japanese-inspired
sum are also on offer

Imperial China
White Bear Yard
25A Lisle Street, wc2
tel. 020 7734 3388
email: info@imperial-china.co.uk
www.imperial-china.co.uk/
Eight vip rooms in this courtyarded
Chinese restaurant tucked away on a
back street in Chinatown. All rooms
are equipped with karaoke machines,
with capacity for parties of up to 30
people. Songs include old classics

Straits Restaurant and Karaoke Bar
5 White Horse Street, w1
tel. 0871 075 1674
www.thestraits.co.uk
A family-run restaurant in Mayfair
specializing in Straits-style food from
Singapore, Malaysia and Thailand.
Private karaoke rooms with their own
bars, for up to 60 people for hire.
Asian style and clients

Karaoke Box Dai Chan
18 Frith Street, w1
tel. 0871 075 1610
This Soho club, one of the first karaoke
clubs in London, is Japanese in style. It
is now considered to be rather old fash-
ioned, although it still attracts Japanese
clients. Has a mixture of Western and
Japanese songs

Village Soho
81 Wardour Street, w1
tel. 020 7434 2124
www.village-soho.co.uk
Opened in 1991 for London's gay community, one of the main attractions

here is the Tuesday Karaoke Forever
Night at its Moroccan style bar

MANCHESTER

Tribeca Bar & BED
50 Sackville Street, M1
www.tribeca-bar.co.uk/
Karaoke on Sunday, gay friendly

The New Union Pub
111 Princess Street/Canal Street, M1
Karaoke night on Wednesday, gay
friendly

Orchid Lounge Karaoke Bar and
Restaurant
52–4 Portland Street, M1
Thai karaoke bar

Thai E-Sarn
210 Burton Road
Didsbury, near Manchester
The owner is an Elvis fan and karaoke
aficionado

PARIS

Nomads
45 Rue Descartes, 75005
www.nomads.fr/

Café Rive Droite
2 Rue Berger, 75002
tel. 01 42 33 81 62

NORTHERN ITALY

Highlander Happy Time
Strada Statale Briantea 5
Palazzago, Bergamo
Organizes karaoke competitions
tel. 035 540451

Biblos
Via Madonnina 17
zona Brera, Milan
tel. 028 051860
A historical bar with karaoke in the
basement

ROME

Karaoke Ko Rio Chung
Via Roma Libera 153
Korean and Chinese restaurant plus
karaoke

MOSCOW

Yanpen Karaoke Lounge
Under Novoye Vremya office behind
the Rossiya Cinema Pushkin Square
Voted one of the best bars in the world,
with a huge selection of songs to choose
from, and it is open from 6 pm until you
leave

TURKEY

ISTANBUL

Karaoke Bar
Nispetiye Caddesi No. 50/2 Etiler
Besiktas
tel. 0 212 458 06 22

к Club
Swissotel the Bosphorus
Bayildim Caddesi 2
Maçka Besiktas
tel. 0212 326 11 00

NORTH AMERICA

NEW YORK

Winnie's
104 Bayard St
10013-4465
tel. 212 732 2384
Reputed to be New York's most entertaining karaoke bar, with rude waiters
and hostesses who cannot make a
decent cocktail. Still widely popular

Asia Roma Bar & Lounge
40 Mulberry St @ Worth St
10013
tel. 212 385 1133
Karaoke where Italy and China
converge, with giant screen and
fancy equipment

Village Karaoke
27 Cooper Sq
10003-7107
tel. 212 254 0066
All-night karaoke for private parties

TORONTO

мнꝗ Karaoke4300 Steeles Ave East
tel. 905 946 9488
Sophisticated hip Karaoke bar, popular
with middle-class Chinese

Melody Bar
The Gladstone Hotel
1241 Queen Street West
tel. 416 531 4635
Voted best karaoke bar by *now
Magazine* for four years, Peter Style
hosts from Thursday through to
Saturday night every week

FLORIDA

Singers Karaoke Klub
3521 NW 8th Ave
Pompano Beach, 33064
tel. 954 785 1945
Boasts it is the 'biggest little karaoke
bar in south Florida', reputed for its
'cosy' and 'intimate' atmosphere

Maria's Mexican Bar & Restaurant
27080 Old US 41, Next to the Wonder
Garden
Bonita Springs, 34135
tel. 239 495 1868
Here you can enjoy karaoke in Spanish,
German and English

Paradise Lakes Resort
PO Box 750
Land O'Lakes, 34639
tel. 813 949 9327
www.paradiselakes.com
Where you can try nude karaoke

LOS ANGELES

Brass Monkey
659 S Mariposa Ave, 90005
tel. 213 381 7047
Hugely popular, so long waits to sing

SOUTH AMERICA

SÃO PAULO

Corcoran
Afonso Brás
657 Vila Nova Conceiçao
www.corcoran.com.br/

CHINA

SHANGHAI

Lang Sha
7F Manhattan Plaza
463 Nanjing Donglu
www.langshaktv.com
You can make your own CD here

Gone Lead
111 Caoxi Lu
(by Caoxi Lu metro station)
Special effects sound system,
free all-you-can-eat buffet

Jinse Niandai
8/F Huaihai Zhonglu
tel. 6467 9999
Don't go there unless someone else
offers to pay

D8 Club
7/F, Lansheng Bldg
8 Huaihai Zhonglu
(near Xizang Nan Lu)
tel. 6319 0837
1920s and '30s atmosphere with a
live band and hundreds of old songs
in Mandarin, Cantonese, English,
Japanese and Korean. A place for
nostalgia and reminiscing

BEIJING

Tangren Jie (New Chinatown)
Jianguomenwai (directly across from
the Guiyou Building)
tel. 6568 3838
Mock Tang dynasty style façade, with
staff as cold and stony as Terracotta
warriors, but still very popular with
young people. Over 60 comfortable
and spacious rooms across from the
courtyard

Melody
Chaoyangmenwai Dajie 77
tel. 6551 0808
Massive building with an open front
bar, great for people watching.
Escalator takes one directly to the
private rooms

Qian Gui (Cash Box)
Full Link Plaza
Chaoyangmenwai
tel. 6588 3333
One of the biggest karaoke chains in
the Chinese-speaking world. It is also
known as Party World. The city's
classiest and best-equipped do-it-
yourself concert venue, it boasts a
hotel-like lobby, pleasantly decorated
private rooms and a wide selection
of Western songs, including many
classics

HONG KONG

V-MIXKaraoke
2-8 Sugar Street, Causeway Bay
tel. 2137 9888

Claims to be the biggest karaoke box in South-east Asia. It is extremely popular, with comfy rooms, cool design, top service and good food. There is even a toilet in each room. It is open from midday until early morning everyday

LHASA

JJ's Disco
People's Park, Southwest side
Opposite the Potala
One of the biggest disco and karaoke venues in the city, with live performers and a mix of love songs and tech lit. A $3 cover charge. There are a number of smaller karaoke bars in the area without a cover charge, though watch out for the hefty price for a bottle of beer

KASHI

Wenzhou Mansion Kashgar
No. 17 Renmin West Road
tel. 86 998 2808889
If any of the karaoke lounges filled with locals in the heart of the city, near the People's Squares, do not strike your fancy, you can always try this one

UZBEKISTAN

KOREANA

73 Nukus Street (at the Koreana Hotel)
Tashkent
tel. 54 25 55, 54 99 45, 54 35 87
Korean food and karaoke
Star Prestige Club
34 Akhunbabaev St.

Tashkent
tel.: 132 1266, 132 1331
European, Uzbek and Korean food to accompany karaoke

JAPAN

TOKYO

Karaoke-kan
Shinjuku area
tel. 03 3346 3488
Shibuya area
tel. 03 3462 0785
Ikebukuro East exit
tel. 03 5957 7566
Kichijoji South exit
tel. 0422 42 1330

For a list of Karaoke-kan in Japanese see gnavi.joy.ne.jp/GN/chain/karaoke.htm#ichiran
A chain-store karaoke lounge with 'boxes', as featured in the film *Lost in Translation*, near almost every major train station

Big Echo
Shibuya area
tel. 03 5458 6341
Shinjuku area
tel. 03 3200 7545
Roppongi area
tel. 03 5411 4898
For a list of Big Echo places (in Japanese) see gnavi.joy.ne.jp/GN/karaoke/bigecho.htm
Another popular chain with 'boxes', also known as 'human song network', it is all over Tokyo

GS Studio
Roppongi Square Building
tel. 03 5411 2301
A karaoke box with a grown-up
atmosphere

Pandora
Kichijoji
tel. 0422 20 8891
A very reasonable karaoke place where
you can bring your own drinks and
food, or pay one price and get all you
can drink

Pop-La
Kichijohi
tel. 0422 21 6928
Also operates an all-you-can-drink
policy for 500 yen per hour per person.

KOREA

SEOUL

Noraebang Luxury
Hongdea area, near Hong-ik
University, no address just ask a local.
Open 24 hours, free ice cream on a
heated floor, with a huge queue in the
early mornings and late evenings

Ben Hur
2F, 13-11 Yeouido-Dong,
Youngdeungpo-Ku, Seoul
tel. 02 783 2233
www.hotelbenhur.com
Large screen, horseshoe seating around
a large table with friendly staff

Singing Room
From Exit #2 of Hyehya Station (Line 4)
go up the side street away from the main
drag past Coffee Bean (on the left) about
three streets. Look for the signpost on
left. Pay $11 per hour with free drinks,
four floors and cool looking, with huge
windows overlooking the street

THAILAND

BANGKOK

SF Music City
Zone D, 7th Floor
MBK Centre
Siam Square
tel. 02 686 3555, 3629
34 karaoke rooms on top of the city's
giant shopping mall. Popular with
young people

44-Entertainment
Chokchai 4, Ladprao Soi 44
tel. 02 931 5321 5
Situated in north Bangkok, 44-
Entertainment offers typical karaoke
format including open lounge and
private VIP booths

Horizons Sky Lounge Karaoke
25th floor
The Westin Grande Sukhumvit
259 Sukhumvit Road
tel. 02 651 1000
More than 5,000 songs and ultra
hi-tech sound system, with magnificent
night views of the city

Tawan Daeng
484 Pattanakarn Road
10250
Popular with Isaan people, with
Morlam music, Isaan-style food and
drinks, up to 300 people turn up on
any given night and there is a big
dancing and singing party for all

Pharaoh's Music Bar
104 Silom Road, Soi 4
tel. 02 234 7249
email: info@pharaohsmusicpub.com
www.pharaohsmusicbar.com
Popular, upscale gay karaoke club
with plush surroundings in a stylish
atmosphere. Some serious singers
and celebrities visit it

References

Introduction

1 '10 Questions for Bob Costas', *Time* (23 August 2004).
2 Frank Hoffmann, 'Lee Bul: Cyborgs and Karaoke: A Traveling Exhibition, Now at the New Museum in New York, Highlights the Recent Karaoke-Based Work of a Korean Artist Known for her High-Tech Feminism and "Global" Fusions of Culture', *Arts in America* (May 2002).
3 Charlie Amter, 'A Real Find: Tokyo of "Lost in Translation"', *San Francisco Chronicle*, 29 February 2004.
4 See Frank Dikötter, *Material Culture and Everyday Life in Modern China* (London, forthcoming).
5 John Urry, 'Complexity Turn', in *Global Complexity* (Cambridge, 2003), pp. 17–38.
6 Interview with Moise Lagos.
7 Michelle Zhang, 'Make Short Work of a Novel', *Shanghai Daily*, 15 September 2005.
8 See www.christianitytoday.com/YC/2004/006/6.44.html (accessed July 2006).
9 See itp.nyu.edu/archive/thesis/spring2005/detail.php?project_id=194 (accessed July 2006).
10 Alain Anciaux, *Karaoké*, available at www.ulb.ac.be/project/feerie/karaoke.html (accessed July 2006).

1 Who Invented Karaoke?

1 See www.lawphil.net/judjuris/juri1996/mar1996/gr_115106_1996.html (accessed July 2006).
2 Toru Mitsui, 'The Genesis of Karaoke', in Toru Mitsui and Shuhei

Hosokawa, eds, *Karaoke around the World: Global Technology, Local Singing* (London and New York, 2001), p. 40.

3 See web-japan.org/nipponia/nipponia12/start.html (accessed July 2006), and Pico Iyer, 'Daisuke Inoue, the Karaoke King', *Time* [Asia], CLVI/78 (23–30 August 1999).

4 Iyer, 'Daisuke Inoue, the Karaoke King'.

5 See *Asahi Shimbun*, 5 October 2004 (IHT/Asahi: 6 October 2004).

6 See David McNeill, 'Mr Song and Dance Man', *Japan Focus*, 22 September 2005. See also David McNeill, 'The Man Who Taught the World to Sing', *The Independent*, 24 May 2006.

7 See en.wikipedia.org//wiki/karaoke (accessed July 2006). Cf. Alain Anciaux, *Karaoké*, available at www.ulb.ac.be/project/feerie/karaoke.html (accessed July 2006), chapter 1, p. 4.

8 See www.karaokescene.com/history (accessed July 2006).

9 See cds.ibcjapan.com/cerddeng.html (accessed July 2006). Cf. Ancieux, *Karaoké*, chapter 1, p. 4.

10 See P. N. Williams, 'The Long Struggle for Identity: The Story of Wales and its People', in www.britannia.com/wales/lit/lit14.html (accessed July 2006).

11 Richard R. Terry, ed., *Gilbert and Sandy's Christmas Carols with Six Collateral Tunes* (London, 1931).

12 For further readings, see Michael Musgave, *The Music Life of the Crystal Palace* (New York, 2005).

13 Nigel Fountain, *Lost Empires* (London, 2006); see also Richard D. Altick, *The Shows of London* (Cambridge, MA, 1978). For a history of popular music and entertainment venues in England and their roots in nineteenth-century social practies, see D. Hashlam, *Manchester, England: The Story of the Pop Cult City* (London, 1999).

14 Yang Jiasheng, 'Dafang guanming de yike liuxing' [The big shining star], in Feng Zhicheng, *Shimin jiyizhong de Lao Chengdu* [Old Chengdu in the memories of locals] (Chengdu, 1999), p. 164.

15 See Iyer, 'Daisuke Inoue, the Karaoke King'.

2 'Karaoke Fever': *Japan and Korea*

1 See Pico Iyer, 'Daisuke Inoue, the Karaoke King', in *Time* [Asia], CLVI/78 (23–30 August 1999).

2 'Closet Carusos', *Time* (28 February 1983).

3 See www.karaokescene.com/history (accessed July 2006).

4 Toru Mitsui, 'The Genesis of Karaoke', in Toru Mitsui and Shuhei

Hosokawa, eds, *Karaoke around the World*, pp. 38–40.

5 'Takako Doi: An Unmarried Woman', *Time* (7 August 1989).

6 'Closet Carusos'.

7 Interview with Mamika, London, 9 October 2005.

8 L. Craft, 'Karaoke Versus Keitai', June 2003,
www.japaninc.net/article.php?articleID=1113 (accessed July 2006).

9 J. Sean Curtin, 'Japan's "Fortress of Solitude" in Iraq – plus Karaoke', *Asia Times*, 19 February 2004.

10 Adam Lebowitz, 'Screaming "Idiot" in the Middle of Iraq', *Asia Times*, 3 July 2004.

11 William Kelly, 'Training for Leisure: *Karaoke* and the Seriousness of Play in Japan', in J. Hendry and M. Raveri, eds, *Japan at Play: The Ludic and the Logic of Power* (London and New York, 2002), p. 153.

12 *Josei Seven* (22 April 1993); trans. in Kelly, 'Training for Leisure', p. 154.

13 'Utai joozu, kiki joozu: kotsu to mana' [Singing well, listening well: tips and manner], in *Shuukan Josei* [Women's Weekly], 17 March 1997, pp. 146–7; see Kelly, 'Training for Leisure'.

14 Kelly, 'Training for Leisure', p. 161.

15 'Man Shot as Karaoke Song Triggers Instant Hit',
www.karaokegoss.com/The_News/Hot_off_the_Karaoke_Goss_presses/Fr
om_Abroad_-_Man_Shot_as_Karaoke_Song_Triggers_Instant_Hit
(accessed July 2006).

16 See www.dogandponysound.com/news_world.htm#news10 (accessed July 2006).

17 Mark Schilling, *The Encyclopedia of Japanese Pop Culture* (New York and Tokyo, 1997), pp. 91–2.

18 For further readings on the subject of Japan and international fairs, see Angus Lockyer, *Japan at the Exhibition, 1862–2005* (forthcoming).

19 Park Moo-jong, 'National Sports', *Korean Times*, 2 November 2002.

20 Ibid.

21 Ken May, 'Anarchy in the S.K.', see www.ajarn.com/Contris/kenmaydecem-ber2004.htm (accessed July 2006).

22 Ibid.

23 Ibid.

24 Heri Lim, 'Let's Go to Karaoke',
oregonstate.edu/~healeyd/sehs/karaoke.html (accessed July 2006).

25 May, 'Anarchy in the S.K.'.

26 Adrienne McGuire, 'Country with Seoul', *Anchorage Press*, 22–8 March 2001.

27 Jonathan Walsh, 'Hit me baby one more time', www.redbrick.dcu.ie/~mel-moth/korea/music.html (accessed July 2006).

28 May, 'Anarchy in the S.K.'.
29 Seo Soo Min, 'Songs of Unification Winning Hearts of People', *Korea Times*, 20 August 2000.

3 Karaoke Wonderland: *South-east Asia*

1 See Cyril Fieve, 'Karaoke Culture', in *Metro* [Thailand], July 2003.
2 See www.jakartaeye.org/flesh_trade.htm (accessed July 2006).
3 See Ruth Rosenburg, ed. 'Traffic Women and Children in Indonesia', at www.solidaritycentre.org/files/IndoTraffickingOverview.pdf, p. 19.
4 See 'Human supply and demand', *Bangkok Post*, 24 April 2005.
5 Ibid. See also Chheang Bopha, 'Cambodia-Thailand: Migrant Villagers Bring Back Worries on AIDS', Inter Press Service, 17 May 2005, at www.aegis.org/news/ips/2005/ip050505.html
6 Fieve, 'Karaoke Culture'.
7 Ibid.
8 See David Tang, 'Jukebox Booth Craze Grips Thailand', *Straits Times*, 16 September 2002.
9 See 'Fun of the Fare', *Bangkok Post*, 12 May 2003.
10 See 'Taxi Offers Free Internet Service', *Bangkok Post*, 26 October 2004.
11 See www.melvindurai.com/cell.htm (accessed July 2006).
12 'Can the Many Different Types of Popular Music around the World Survive Globalization?', interview with Hiroshi Matsumara, *Asia-Pacific Perspectives*, March 2005.
13 Ibid. See also Amporn Jirattikorn, 'Lukthung: Authenticity and Modernity in Thai Country Music', *Asia Music* (Winter-Spring 2006), pp. 24–49.
14 See www.geocities.com/koratmahknut/IsaanKaraoke/tipsonisaan Karaoke.htm.
15 See Simon Elegant, 'People's Power', *Time* [Asia], 21 June 2004.
16 See http://www.rdic.org/studiopage.htm
17 RDI Cambodia can be contacted via P.O. Box 494, Phnom Penh, Cambodia (www.rdic.org).
18 Eric Bram, 'Cambodia Karaoke', www.travelblog.org, posted 6 June 2004.
19 Ingo Stoevesandt, 'Traditional Music in Cambodia', available on www.istov.de (accessed July 2006).
20 From Mon News, Independent Mon News Agency, 27 January 2003.
21 See Ko Jay, 'Karaoke Nights', *The Irrawaddy* (May 2005).
22 See Lucy Murray, 'Myanmar's Lesson in "Discipline Democracy"', *Asia Times*, 17 February 2005.
23 Celena Cipriaso, '10 Things You Didn't Know about Filipinos';

original posted on AsianAvenue.com.

24 *Philippine Star*, 2 May 2003.

25 Ted Lerner, *The Traveler and the Gate Checkers* (Moreno Valley, CA, 2003).

26 'Our Man in Philippines', *Wessex Scene*, 8 November 2003.

27 Arthur Dun-ping Mak and C. M. Leong, 'Karaoke Therapy in the Rehabilitation of Mental Patients', *Singapore Medical Journal*, XLIII/12 (2002), p. 643.

28 Mark Huy Lê, 'The Role of Music in Second Language Learning: A Vietnamese Perspective', University of Tasmania, paper presented at the Combined 1999 Conference of the Australian Association for Research in Education and the New Zealand Association for Research in Education.

29 Ibid.

30 Nguyen Nam Phuong, 'Patriotic Tunes Fade out as Vietnam Goes Pop', *Asia Times*, 8 January 2000.

31 Robert Olen Butler, 'Saigon', in *Condé Nast Traveler*, October 1995.

32 Marguerite Jordan, 'Complex Images of Vietnam: Khe Sanh, Confucius, Quang Ganh and Karaoke', *Travel Lady Magazine*, no. 54 (2001).

4 The Disneyland of Karaoke Palaces: *China*

1 *World Press Review*, XLIV/8.

2 See Ian Buruma, *Bad Elements: Chinese Rebels from Los Angeles to Beijing* (London, 2001), p. 298.

3 We are grateful to Poppy Sebag Montefiore for introducing us to Chen Xiuhong.

4 'What's a Sing-along Video Worth?', *China Daily*, 24 March 2004.

5 For further readings see George B. Lee, '"The East Is Red" Goes Pop: Commodification, Hybridity and Nationalism in Chinese Popular Song and its Tele-visual Performance', *Popular Music*, XIV/1 (1995), pp. 95–110.

6 The quotation is taken *verbatim* from *Shanghai Duolun Exhibition of Young Artists*, exh. cat., Duolun Museum, October 2004.

7 We are grateful to K. for showing us around karaoke venues in Shanghai. On the relationship between karaoke and prostitution in China in the late 1990s, see also Andrew Higgins, 'Straight on for China and Karaoke Slavery', *The Observer*, 15 March 1998.

8 The following is based on the introduction to E. Jeffreys, *China, Sex and Prostitution: Telling Tales* (London and New York, 2004).

9 Nury Vittachi, *Travellers' Tales* (Hong Kong, 1994), p. 49

10 David Wu, 'Local Party Scene', *City Weekend*, 9–22 December 2004, p. 24.

11 We are grateful to Anna for letting us use her story.

5 Karaoke for the Soul: *Karaoke and Religion*

1 See lifestyle.iafrica.com/brain_food/bf_features/400173.htm (accessed July 2006).

2 Ibid., and www.khmer.org/product/0,prod,0,0,0,2283,0.htm (accessed July 2006).

3 See 'Crooning Monk Defrocked in Cambodia', *Asian Reporter*, 17 May 2005, pp. 2–3.

4 See 'Karaoke Monk Booted out', BBC News, 20 October 2000, news.bbc.co.uk/hi/world/asia-pacific/982094.stm.

5 See C. Sanham, 'The Show Goes on for Thai Media and Monk Circus', *Asia Times*, 20 October 2001.

6 Personal communication with Yoke Voon, London, May 2004.

7 See S. Chandler, *Establishing a Pure Land on Earth: The Foguang Buddhist Perspective on Modernization and Globalization* (Honolulu, 2004); for BLIA's history and activities see especially pp. 126–7, 191–4, 264–7.

8 For further discussion of these phenomena, see F. Tarocco, 'Re-tuning the Dharma: Issues on the Popularisation of Buddhist Music in China', *Audiences, Patrons and Performers in the Performing Arts of Asia, International Institute for Asian Studies Conference: Leiden, 21 August 2000*, CHIME *Journal*, 14–15 (2000), pp. 192–3.

9 See Daniel Yeo's website www.buddhanet.net/audio-songs_chinese.htm (accessed July 2006).

10 See L. D. Reed, 'Song of Myself, on Tape: Japanese Sound-blending Machines are Making US Melodies', *Time*, 15 July 1985, p. 74.

11 J. Prichard, 'Christian Karaoke Music Finds Niche', *Columbia Chronicle Online*, 6 January 2003: www.ccchronicle.com/back/2003_spring/2003-01-06/arts8.html (accessed July 2006).

12 See A. H. Lee, 'Christian Karaoke Sales Bounce Higher', *The Christian Post*, at www.christianpost.com/article/general/167/fall/christian.karaoke.sales.bounce.higher/1.htm/, (accessed June 2005).

13 Prichard, 'Christian Karaoke Music Finds Niche'.

14 *Daily Telegraph*, 24 May 2001.

15 See www.bbc.co.uk/commissioning/tv/network/genres/arts_strands.shtml (accessed July 2006).

16 See 'Islamic State Bans Karaoke', BBC News, 6 June 2000, news.bbc.co.uk/1/hi/world/asia-pacific/780081.stm (accessed July 2006).

6 'Naked Karaoke' and the Cowboys: *North America*

1 See www.ryanrowe.com/imba/20041030.html (accessed July 2006).

2 See www.dogandponysound.com/news_world.htm#healey (accessed July 2006).

3 For more information on the Toronto Karaoke Meetup Group, see www.karaoke.meetup.com (accessed July 2006).

4 See japanese.meetup.com/28/events/?eventId=4386871&action=pastdetail (accessed July 2006).

5 See www.rambles.net/mills_kcowboy03.html (accessed July 2006).

6 See www.trevormills.com/bio.php (accessed July 2006). Cf. Angela Page, 'Trevor Mills: Karaoke Cowboy', *Sing Out! The Folk Song Magazine* (Fall 2003).

7 For further information see www.peterstyles.info (accessed July 2006).

8 Donna Lypchuk, 'Seven Laws of Karaoke', *Eye Weekly*, 2 March 2000.

9 See William Chun, 'Toronto Asia Karaoke and Karaoke Bars', *Institute for Canadian Music Newsletter*, II/1 (January 2004), pp. 7–9. For further readings on Karaoke and Asian communities in North America see Rob Drew, *Karaoke Nights: An Ethnographic Rhapsody* (Walnut Creek, CA, 2001); M. K. Casey Lum, *In Search of a Voice: Karaoke and the Construction of Identity in Chinese America* (Mahwah, NJ, 1996); D. Wong, 'I Want the Microphone: Mass Mediation and Agency in Asian-American Popular Music', *Drama Review*, XXXVIII/3 (1994), pp. 152–67.

10 See discorder.citr.ca/features/05mayporn.html (accessed July 2006).

11 See the article at www.guardian.co.uk/uk_news/story/0,3604,1366188,00.html (accessed July 2006).

12 See Montrealmirror.com/ARCHIVES/2002/102402/nightlife3.html

13 Ibid.

14 See www.karaokegonewild.com (accessed July 2006).

15 See www.singerskaraoke.com. (accessed August 2006).

16 See www.davelessnau.com. (accessed August 2006).

17 See www.cnn.com/WORLD/fringe/9608/17/naked.karaoke (accessed July 2006).

18 See www.newsmax.com/archives/articles/2003/9/3/115146.shtml (accessed January 2006). Also see the Epilogue below concerning North Korea.

19 See www.extremeachievers.com/karaoke.htm

20 See www.asianweek.com/2002_11_08/arts_karaoke.html (accessed July 2006).

21 See http://citypaper.com/clubs/story.asp?id=9179 (accessed August 2006).

22 Ben Fong-Torres, 'Karaoke: "There's Always Someone Worse than You Are"', *The City* (September 1992); available at www.benfongtorres. com/asianconnections/karaoke/karaoke.html (accessed July 2006).

23 Rick Harrison, 'Keeping Songs Alive – with Karaoke', *The Forward*, 18 March 2005; available at www.forward.com/articles/2854 (accessed July 2006).

24 Diccon Hyatt, 'Middletown Karaoke Champ Headed to Nationals'; available at www.middletowntranscript.com/TransArchives/05-06-04/pages/karaoke.html (accessed July 2006).

7 The Karaoke Nation: *Britain*

1 See elt.britcoun.org.pl/elt/i_quote.htm (accessed August 2006).

2 See 'Take a Chance on me', www.gamblingmagazine.com/articles/32/32-163.htm (accessed July 2006).

3 See www.drownedinsound.com/articles/13060.html (accessed July 2006).

4 See www.dogandponysound.com/news_world.htm#news6 (accessed July 2006).

5 See Institute of Policy Research, *Public Houses* (London, 2002).

6 For further readings on karaoke and English singing tradition. see William Kelly, 'The Adaptability of Karaoke in the United Kingdom', in Toru Mitsui and Shuhei Hosokawa, eds, *Karaoke around the World: Global Technology, Local Singing* (London and New York, 2001), pp. 83–101.

7 See Dennis Potter, *Karaoke and Cold Lazarus* (London, 1996), p. 95.

8 Interview with Dennis Potter, Channel Four Television, broadcast 5 April 1994.

9 Conrad de Aenlle, 'Now, a Karaoke in Every Home?', *International Herald Tribune*, 24 April 1992.

10 Jess Cartner-Morley, 'Step up to the Mic . . .', *The Guardian*, 20 June 2005.

11 See www.dogandponysound.com/news_world.htm (accessed July 2006).

8 'Karaoke Forever': *Europe*

1 Among the existing research on karaoke, Alain Anciaux's *Karaoké*, an e-book available at www.ulb.ac.be/project/feerie/karaoke.html (accessed July 2006), is of particular value. Other studies on karaoke in Europe can be found in Toru Mitsui and Shuhei Hosokawa, eds, *Karaoke around the World*. See also Chapters 5, 7 and 10 of this volume.

2 Personal communication, London, September 2003.

3 See especially Chapters 1, 2, 3 and 7 in Anciaux, *Karaoké*, which contains many examples of karaoke social practices in Belgium and France.

4   For some discussion of these matters, see Y. Salmandjee and S. Lecomte, *Le karaoke (tout savoir pour chanter chez soi ou dans des lieux publics)* (Paris, 2003).

5   See, for instance, 'Karastar' at www.ulb.ac.be/project/feerie/phomois.html (accessed July 2006); see also the section on 'Nikkei karaoke'.

6   Anciaux, *Karaoké*, Chapter 1, p. 18.

7   See *L'Officiel des spectacles*, 30 June–6 July 2004, pp. 137–8.

8   Personal communication, Montpellier, July 2004.

9   Fiorello's interview appeared in the magazine *QN*, 18 January 2004.

10   See P. Prato, 'From TV to Holidays: Karaoke in Italy', in Mitsui and Hosokawa, eds, *Karaoke around the World*, pp. 102–17 [p. 106].

11   G. Pansa, 'Videomessaggio e karaoke, così iniziò l'era del Cavaliere', *La Repubblica*, 23 January 2004. Translated by the authors.

12   C. De Gregorio, '"Credo laico" e elicotteri al congresso del karaoke', *La Repubblica*, 28 May 2004. Translated by the authors.

13   '*Top of the Pops* Breaks Records in Italy', posted 1 April 2004, www.bbc.co.uk/ pressoffice/commercial/worldwidestories/pressreleases/2004/htm.

14   See especially Prato, 'From TV to Holidays: Karaoke in Italy', pp. 112–15.

15   The story, called 'L'inferno è un karaoke' or 'Hell is a karaoke', is found at buonipresagi.splinder.com/archive/2005-05 (accessed July 2006).

16   Note that many Italian websites that offered free downloadable material have been forced to withdraw it. On Italian websites, see also chapter Ten below.

17   This site can no longer be accessed. The URL was www.emimusic.it/web/ forum_detail.asp?id_message=8393&category=1 (accessed August 2004).

18   Personal communications, Milan, Padua and Rome, August 2004.

19   Interview with Silvia Barna, August 2005.

20   Personal communications. See also www.come2clubmed.com/otranto.htm (accessed July 2006).

21   Cf. the Finnish website www.karaoket.com (accessed July 2006). For an account of Swedish karaoke culture, see J. Fornas, 'Filling Voids along the Byway: Identification and Interpretation in the Swedish Forms of Karaoke', in Mitsui and Hosokawa, eds, *Karaoke around the World*, pp. 118–38.

22   Cf. kwcusa.com and www.khviihde.fi/kwcgallery (both accessed July 2006).

23   See the article 'Wife-Carrying Championship: Tradition marries sports and fun in the annual Wife-Carrying World Championships celebrated in the town of Sonkajärvi, Finland, between the 2nd and 4th July 2004', www.scandinavica.com/culture/sports/wife.htm (accessed July 2006).

24   See ec.europa.eu/education/programmes/socrates/comenius/week03/ workshop7_en.html (accessed July 2006).

9 Karaoke in Brazil: *The Nikkeijin Story*

1 See T. Tsuda, 'The Benefits of being Minority: the Ethnic Status of the Japanese-Brazilians in Brazil', *The Centre for Comparative Immigration Study, University of California, San Diego*, Working Paper 21 (May 2000), p. 6.

2 Ibid., p. 11.

3 S. Hosokawa, 'Singing in a Cultural Enclave', in Toru Mitsui and Shuhei Hosokawa, eds, *Karaoke around the World: Global Technology, Local Singing* (London and New York, 1998), p. 142.

4 See the materials in the official site of the Japanese television channel NHK, www.nhk.or.jp/ (accessed July 2006).

5 See Shuhei Hosokawa, 'Singing not Together: Karaoke in São Paulo', in W. Straw and others, eds, *Popular Music – Style and Identity: Proceedings of the 7th Conference of the International Association for the Study of Popular Music* (Montreal, 1995), p. 151.

6 Cf. Shuhei Hosokawa, 'Singing in a Cultural Enclave', in Toru Mitsui and Shuhei Hosokawa, eds, *Karaoke around the World*, pp. 145–7.

7 *Wall Street Journal*, 11 February 1998.

8 See Cf. D. de Carvalho, 'The Making of a Minority in Japan', *Japan Foundation Newsletter*, XXVII/3–4 (2000), p. 19.

9 Ibid., p. 20.

10 See the ethnographic materials collected in 'Nikkei Identity in Oizumi Japan', available at www.conncoll.edu/academics/departments/transnat/luis/nightlife.html (accessed July 2005).

11 M. K. Casey Lum, *In Search of a Voice: Karaoke and the Construction of Identity in Chinese America* (Mahwah, NJ, 1996), p. 1.

10 Karaoke Revolution: *Karaoke Technologies*

1 See Conrad de Aenlle, 'Now, a Karaoke in Every Home', *International Herald Tribune*, 24 April 1992.

2 J. Legon, 'Microphone Brings Karaoke Home', www.CNN.com, 9 December 2002, available at www.cnn.com/2002/TECH/ptech/12/04/sproject.hso2.karaoke.mike/index.html (accessed July 2006).

3 Quoted in D. Wong, 'I Want the Microphone: Mass Mediation and Agency in Asian-American Popular Music', *Drama Review*, XXXVIII/3 (1994), p. 157, also pp. 152–67.

4 Mark Schilling, *The Encyclopedia of Japanese Pop Culture* (New York and Tokyo, 1997), p. 90.

5   C. de Aenlle, 'Now, a Karaoke in Every Home'.

6   Lev Grossman, 'Toys that Twist and Shout', *Time*, 18 February 2002.

7   J. Gudmundsen, 'Kids Get Jump Start with Karaoke Software', *Home News Tribune*, 16 August 2005.

8   P. Lockheart, 'A History of Early Microphone Singing, 1925–1939: American Mainstream Popular Singing at the Advent of Electronic Microphone Amplification', *Popular Music and Society*, XXVI/3 (2003), p. 381.

9   Alain Anciaux, personal communication, 17 March 2005.

10   J. Legon, 'Microphone Brings Karaoke Home'.

11   See *Japan Close-Up*, October 2004, p. 24. Cf. also www.toynes.jp/summer/takara/ekaramix.htm (accessed August 2005).

12   E. Lewis, 'Karaoke Revolution – the Revolution will be Televised', available at ps2.ign.com/articles/458/458064p1.html (accessed July 2006).

13   Cf. corp.eatsleepmusic.com (accessed July 2006).

14   A fairly up-to-date compilation of hundreds of web pages (mostly in French) devoted to all aspect of karaoke can be found in chapter 9 of the e-book *Karaoké* by the anthropologist and karaoke practitioner Alain Anciaux, also known in karaoke circles by his pseudonym 'Doctor Al'; available at www.ulb.ac.be/project/feerie/karaoke.html (accessed July 2006).

15   See www.wainer.com/ (accessed July 2006).

16   See the specialist website www.gamespy.com, available at archive.gamespy.com/articles/july03/famicom/index7.shtml.

17   Jess Cartner-Morley, 'Step up to the Mic', *The Guardian*, 20 June 2005.

18   E. Lewis, 'Karaoke Revolution – the Revolution will be Televised'.

19   Lucille Craft, 'Karaoke versus *Keitai*', *Japan Inc. News*, June 2003; available at www.japaninc.net/article.php?articleID=1113 (accessed July 2006).

20   S. Dodson, 'Where the Mobile is Killing the PC', *The Guardian*, 17 April 2003.

21   See the industry website www.ringtonia.com, available at www.textually.org/ringtonia/archives/2003/10/001987.htm (accessed July 2006).

22   See 'Mobile Karaoke Rocks Russia', *St Petersburg Times*, 26 April 2005.

23   See 'The Latest in Mobile Content – Karaoke', www.CNET.com, 17 October 2003 (accessed September 2005).

24   See Singapore's 2005 National Day website, available at www.ndp.org.sg/index.jsp?page=Mobile/karaoke.htm (accessed August 2005).

Epilogue: *Karaoke at the Frontiers*

1   See Nury Vittachi, *Travellers' Tales* (Hong Kong, 1994), p. 40.

2   See Vivienne Adams, 'Karaoke as Modern Lhasa, Tibet: Western Encounters

with Cultural Politics', *Cultural Anthropology*, XI/4 (2004), pp. 510–46
3   See M. A. Sheldon, 'Report from Tibet: China's Undercover War on Religious Life', *World Tibet Network News*, 9 November 1993.
4   See Adams, 'Karaoke as Modern Lhasa, Tibet', pp. 510, 512 and 514.
5   Pepe Escobar, 'Silk Road Roving', *Asia Times*, 1 November 2003.
6   'Karaoke in North Korean Shipment', BBC News, 3 January 2001.

Select Bibliography

Adams, V., 'Karaoke as Modern Lhasa, Tibet: Western Encounters with Cultural
Politics', *Cultural Anthropology*, XI/4 (2004), pp. 510–46
Anciaux, Alain, *Karaoké*, e-book available at
www.ulb.ac.be/project/feerie/karaoke.html (accessed July 2006)
Drew, Rob, *Karaoke Nights: An Ethnographic Rhapsody* (Walnut Creek, CA, 2001)
Hendry, J., and M. Raveri, eds, *Japan at Play: The Ludic and the Logic of Power*
(London and New York, 2002)
Lockheart, P., 'A History of Early Microphone Singing, 1925–1939: American
Mainstream Popular Singing at the Advent of Electronic Microphone
Amplification', *Popular Music Society*, XXVF/3 (2003), pp. 367–85
Lum, Man Kong Casey, *In Search of a Voice: Karaoke and the Construction of Identity in
Chinese America* (Mahwah, NJ, 1996)
Mitsui, Toru, and Shuhei Hosokawa, eds, *Karaoke around the World: Global
Technology, Local Singing* (London and New York, 2001)
Porter, D., *Karaoke and Cold Lazarus* (London, 1996)
Salmandjee, Y., and S. Lecomte, *Le karaoke* (*tout savoir pour chanter chez soi ou dans
des lieux publics*) (Paris, 2003)
Schilling, Mark, *The Encyclopedia of Japanese Pop Culture* (New York and Tokyo, 1997)
Straw, W., and others, eds, *Popular Music – Style and Identity: Proceedings of the
7th Conference of the International Association for the Study of Popular Music*
(Montreal, 1995)
Urry, John, *Global Complexity* (Cambridge, 2003)
Wong, D., 'I Want the Microphone: Mass Mediation and Agency in Asian-American
Popular Music', *The Drama Review*, XXXVIII/3 (1994), pp. 152–67

Photos and Acknowledgements

The authors and publishers wish to express their thanks to the below sources of illustrative material and/or permission to reproduce it.

Photo ABS-CBN Interactive 2004: p. 79; photo © 2006 Andy Volk: p. 86; photo Antoine D'Agata/Magnum Photos: p. 72; photo Avery Morrow: p. 14; photo Badtz Maru: p. 39 (top right); photo Brandon Daniel: p. 32; photo Carl De Keyzer/Magnum Photos: p. 17 (top); photo © Carmen Martínez Banús/2006 iStock International Inc.: p. 6; photos Chien-Chi Chang/Magnum Photos: pp. 58, 84; photo Chris Bracken: p. 41; photo Chris Lechner: p. 27 (left); photos Chu Hui Cha: pp. 49, 50; photo Corey Wang: p. 125; photo Dante Higgins: p. 134 (top); photo Daphne Chong: p. 39 (top left); photo David McNeill/Japan Focus (japanfocus.org): p. 21; photo Devonie: p. 132; photo Enrique A Gómez Zermeño: p. 8; photo Erik Delvigne: p. 25; photo Francesca Tarocco: p. 150; photo Geoff Alexander: p. 69; photo Ghazali Bunari: p. 87; photo Gina Zycher: p. 40; photos Gueorgui Pinkhassov/Magnum Photos: pp. 103, 104, 105; photo Gustaf Wallen: p. 75; photo HHW: p. 94; photo H. L. Wang: p. 88; photo Ian Loydi: p. 66; photo Jan Morén: p. 42; photo Jared Maliga: p. 45; photo John Stanmeyer VII for TIME Asia: p. 70; photo John Vink/Magnum Photos: p. 85; photo © 2000-2006 Jornal Nippo Brasil: p. 162; photo Jose Luis Hernandez: p. 13; photo Karalee Brugman: p. 39 (foot); photo © 2006 khmer.org: p. 109; photo KJ Subz: p. 9 (foot); photos © 2006 Konami Digital Entertainment: p. 174 (left); photo Kungfu Tofu: p. 9 (top); photo Laura Thomas: p. 37; photo: Lise Sarfati/Magnum Photos: p. 102; photo Luca Conti: p. 153; photo Mary Frances Capiello: p. 100; photos Mihai Peteu: p. 163; photo M. R. Leaman/Reaktion Books: p. 16; photo courtesy of Lucky Voice: pp. 15, 143; photos Patrick Zachmann/Magnum Photos: pp. 73, 91, 92, 93, 101; photo Ren Kuroda: p. 33; photos Rex Features: pp. 28 (Rex Features/LEHTIKUVA OY, 196225A), 29 (Rex Features/Peter Macdiarmid, 189998I), 30 (Rex Features/Sutton-Hibbert, 415510AA), 38 (Rex Features/Roy Garner, 574372L), 63 (Rex Features/Rainer Krack, 151693B), 64

(Rex Features/Rainer Krack (151693C), 106 (Rex Features/Ricky Wong, 460507X), 133 (Charles Sykes/Rex Features, 381533X), 149 (Patrick Frilet/Rex Features, 504046A); photo Reetta Haarajoki: p. 157; photo Rhodri Jones: p. 26; photo Rick and Kathy Wilson: p. 46; photo Robert Benjamin John: p. 27 (right); photo SenorAnderson: p. 134 (foot); photos Silvia Barna: pp. 155, 156; photo © 2003 SingZing.com: p. 114; photo used by courtesy of Stefan Hendrickx: p. 144; photo Stefan Ufer: p. 141; photo Stephen Viller (http://www.flickr.com/photos/viller/): p. 167; photo Thomas: p. 44; photo Trevor Mills (www.trevormills.com): p. 122; photo V. Sergeev: p. 17 (foot); photo William Danskine: p. 152; photo Zhang Zhi: p. 145.

The authors are extremely grateful to a number of people and friends who have made invaluable contributions to this book. Their generous support has made this book possible. We have also made extensive use of material available on the world wide web, and we would like to extend our gratitude to all the authors of the web pages we have consulted. A grant from the Sino-British Fellowship Trust enabled the authors to carry out a reasearch trip to China.

Index